A PASSION FOR BAKING
JO WHEATLEY

Jo Wheatley
A Passion for Baking

CONSTABLE

For Richard and my boys: my reasons for baking

Constable & Robinson Ltd
55–56 Russell Square
London WC1B 4HP
www.constablerobinson.com

First published in the UK by Constable,
an imprint of Constable & Robinson Ltd, 2012

Text copyright © Jo Wheatley, 2012
Photographs © Martin Poole, 2012
Photograph on page 6 © Colin Bell, 2012

The right of Jo Wheatley to be identified
as the author of this work has been asserted
by her in accordance with the Copyright,
Designs and Patents Act 1988

A copy of the British Library Cataloguing
in Publication Data is available from the
British Library

ISBN: 9781-7-8033-856-9 (hardback)

Design & art direction: Smith & Gilmour
Food stylist: Annie Rigg
Prop stylist: Wei Tang

Printed and bound in the EU

1 3 5 7 9 10 8 6 4 2

INTRODUCTION

For me it all started at the tender old age of three, making pastry with my nan in her kitchen on an upturned sock bin. I wonder now, if my nan hadn't allowed me to 'help', would my love of baking have been so intense? My Auntie Helen is also a wonderful baker, and whenever we went over to her place she was always knocking up something amazing. I always wanted just to stand beside her and revel in the homely feeling she created. When my cousin was very small we were invited to his birthday party and Helen made biscuits for all the children with our names piped on them. Luke is nearly forty now and I still remember being in awe of these amazing bakes, iced in pink for the girls and blue for the boys. Even then I knew the love and attention my auntie had put into these little biscuits. On my lovely Dad's side all the aunties and grandchildren used to meet up after a trip to the market every Saturday. There were eight aunties and lots of grandchildren and we all squeezed into my Nanny Jessie's small kitchen, where somebody always had a bag with a bake in it.

Showing a child how to bake can be a lovely experience for both pupil and teacher, perhaps especially when it leads on to a picnic in the garden. My lovely mum-in-law Kath taught me that what children want most is our time. When the boys were little I'd go to collect them and they would all be sat in Kath's garden around a small child's table set for tea – a big mud pie with a candle plonked in the middle of it, three muddy boys, best china and Nanny at the centre of a teddy bears' birthday tea.

Baking is about memories, old ones and ones yet to be made: a favourite auntie's bread pudding; a nan's apple pie; eating the most amazing croissant with a loved one; madeleines that remind you of the most romantic dinner; a birthday cake shaped like a fort for a special four-year-old ... I could go on forever! I'd love to know all your baking memories and hope that *A Passion for Baking* will bring you lots more.

I really try to think of everything when I start to develop a recipe in my mind. First and foremost the flavour. It needs to be balanced: sometimes you need just a little backnote of salt or lemon sharpness to balance that creamy sweetness, or a little coconut to melt into the background of the zesty orangeness. Then the texture – a heavy bake isn't satisfying to anyone (there is nothing worse than wasting calories on a disappointingly heavy bake!). Next is the appearance. Of course we 'eat' with our eyes first, so it must look good. Finally, there's the nose: good baking smells so homely!

I love baking and particularly all the experimenting that goes with it. I have taken to waking up at 3 a.m. with ideas, so now I have a pad by the bed to jot down my nocturnal inspiration. Baking gives me a passion and a creativity that I truly never thought existed, and I love the way it draws people together through their common interest in something so nurturing and giving.

I really am so excited to share my recipes with you. I hope you enjoy baking them as much as I have enjoyed creating them. It's so unbelievable to me that this has all happened, a dream come true. I keep expecting a tap on the shoulder to say it isn't so!

JO'S STORE CUPBOARD

I think it's really necessary to have a well-stocked store cupboard, then at a whim I can knock up something lovely. Every week I buy about half a dozen packets of **unsalted Lurpak butter** – no other brand makes my buttercream as light and fluffy and I have tried lots. The next on my list of essentials is **Stork margarine**, to which I was introduced by Mary Berry. It gives the most wonderfully light texture, which is really important to baking. Also essential is **flour**: of course you need both self-raising and plain, but I think it's always good to have a strong white bread flour as well, and some **fast-acting yeast sachets** (these were recommended to me by the bread master himself, Mr Hollywood). **Eggs** are another must: I keep mine at room temperature in a big bowl, and I always make a point of putting the oldest on top every time I refill.

You must also have plenty of **sugar**. The top three are caster, soft brown and demerara, but never forget icing sugar, of which I always have shelves full so that at any moment I can turn my kitchen into a scene from Johnson's baby powder factory. I also make up little jars of home-made **flavoured sugars**: lavender, cardamom, lemon grass and the one I use most frequently, vanilla.

Also indispensable are **baking powder**, **bicarbonate of soda**, **cream of tartar**, and **vanilla**, paste, extract (never essence) and bean pods.

I use loads of **chocolate** in my cooking – white, milk and dark – but keeping stock at the requisite level is a total nightmare because my boys know where I keep it. Many's the time I've gone to bake and found the cupboard empty of everything other than **cocoa powder**, another must-have item.

My cupboards contain a wide variety of **sprinkles** and **fondant icing**: you can get an amazing selection from supermarkets nowadays. There's also **Dr Oetker cake release spray**, which I've only recently discovered and now would never be without. **Gel colours** are great for colouring cakes and icing of all types: you need such a small amount that they don't change your bake consistency at all. My three main spices are **nutmeg**, **cinnamon** and **mixed ground spice**, but I also love the warming flavour of **cardamom**. **Oranges** and **lemons** are always needed for zest, and because I love fruit I also keep dried **cranberries** and **apricots**: these are every bit as important to a great bake as the staple **currants**, **sultanas** and **raisins**.

You should never run out of **nuts** – principally ground almonds, but also pecans and hazelnuts. As I look around my kitchen I see a pot of **mixed peel**, which I blend to a paste along with **dried fruits**. For flavouring I love **Camp essence** and **Chambord**. I always have two bottles of **oil**, one non-virgin olive, the other sunflower. There's also **buttermilk** and **full-fat Philadelphia**, which should be bought when it's on special offer as it lasts for ages.

As I complete my 360-degree sweep of my work area I notice **cornflour**, which is fantastic for making sponges lighter and thickening sauces, and last but by no means least **rock salt**: you wouldn't believe how much a pinch enhances your bake.

BAKING EQUIPMENT

The list of possible items of baking equipment is almost endless but this is a selection of the essentials and some of the great things I've discovered along the way. Delia Smith once said that you should buy the best you can afford, and I've always stuck by that: the better the baking tray or cake tin, the more even the bake. I always look out for when bakeware is on special offer and buy it then.

I have a whole host of **baking trays**. I have a couple that fit perfectly into my oven for maximum space when making cookies.

A **silicon spatula** is amazing at getting every last bit of batter from the bowl, but it's not so good for the bowl licker.

A **microplane zester** produces more zest from a single fruit than can be obtained using any other implement.

Digital scales make life much easier and minimize the margin of error.

An **oven thermometer** is imperative: the built-in indicators are seldom reliable and accuracy is essential to top-class baking.

A **free-standing mixer**: I know it's expensive, but if you buy a good one it should last almost a baking lifetime and it's a real investment.

Food processor: I use mine daily; it's so good for pastry and biscuits, chopping nuts, fruits and vegetables.

Cake tins: I mainly use a good set of sandwich tins, 20cm (8 inches) and 15cm (6 inches) in diameter, round tins, a Swiss roll tin and a 20 x 20cm (8 x 8-inch) tin for brownies.

Muffin tins: great for cupcakes, orange spiced rolls, popovers and Yorkshire puddings.

Ice-cream scoops: I have two, one large, one small; they are excellent for making uniform-size cookies and for distributing cupcake batter equally into the cases.

Piping bags: I use the disposable variety because I find that the cloth ones always stay greasy.

Wilton 1M: a great nozzle that makes beautiful swirls every time; if I could own only one nozzle, this would be it.

Measuring spoons: mine are shaped so they fit into spice jars.

Baking beans: important for a nice blind bake to stop the pastry rising in the centre.

Sandwich bags: for lustre dusting and for makeshift piping bags; to make fondant rose petals in.

Wire racks for cooling are a must; I never seem to have enough of them.

Wooden spoons for beating butter and sugar.

Offset spatula for spreading buttercream over cakes.

Sieve: great for purées and for dusting icing sugar if you don't have a dredger.

A **cake tester**: takes away the worry of cutting into an underbaked sponge; easy to find on the Internet.

Chapter one

BREAKFAST

I like nothing better than a lazy weekend breakfast.
Sometimes it's so nice to read the newspaper with a
large pot of tea, a big thick slice of a toasted bloomer
or a bowl of steaming porridge with a sticky baked
banana chopped into it. All served and enjoyed in
a solitude that is hard to find in a house like mine.
When the boys were small, if Richard and I had an
evening out, my lovely mum-in-law Kath would have
the children overnight … Oh my, that quiet stillness
in the morning was actually better than a lie-in!

GRANOLA

With granola as with most things, I think it's all about personal choice. You may love pecans and cranberries and not like raisins; alternatively, you may love the flavour of coconut, which to others may be the worst taste in the world. So what I'm going to do is give you the basis of an idea, but I tell you once you've had the home-made variety you will wonder how you ever liked the shop-bought stuff.

300g rolled oats
4 heaped tbsp regular shop-bought apple sauce
4 heaped tbsp clear/runny honey
1 tbsp golden/maple syrup
3 tbsp oil (sunflower or non-virgin olive oil)
60g soft dark brown sugar (or light if you prefer)
4 heaped tbsp desiccated coconut
60g mixed nuts (I love almonds, hazelnuts and pecans), roughly chopped
100g dried fruits (apricots, cherries, raisins, cranberries, pineapple piece, anything you like really), chopped

Preheat the oven to 170°C/325°F/Gas Mark 3.

Mix all the ingredients together, except for the dried fruit, in a large roomy bowl. Make sure that the oats are well coated in the honey, syrup and oil.

Turn the mixture out into a large baking tray in a single layer; shake the tray slightly so that you have some clumps and some smaller bits.

Bake on the middle shelf of the preheated oven for about 35–40 minutes until golden. You will need to keep stirring and jiggling the granola around while it bakes so that it browns evenly.

Once baked, remove from the oven, add the chopped dried fruits and stir to combine. Leave to cool completely and then store in an airtight container. It will keep for a good month.

GRANOLA MUFFINS

*I find muffins such a comforting food, and they are so simple.
Nigella Lawson totally converted me. I love that you can weigh out the
dry ingredients into a bowl and the wet ingredients into a jug before going
to bed, then it's all systems go the next morning. Serve with unsalted butter
and a big cup of coffee. (Obviously no coffee for the kiddies: mine were
always lively enough on fresh juice.)*

250g self-raising flour
½ tsp bicarbonate of soda
180g soft brown sugar
225g granola
220ml full-fat milk
90g unsalted butter, melted
1 large egg

Topping
30g demerara sugar
60g desiccated coconut

**You will need a 12-hole muffin
tin and paper muffin cases**

Preheat the oven to 190°C/375°F/Gas Mark 5.
Line a 12-hole muffin tin with paper muffin cases.

Combine the flour, bicarbonate of soda, soft
brown sugar and granola in a large mixing bowl.

Whisk the milk, melted butter and egg in a jug
until thoroughly combined. Lightly fold into the
dry ingredients but don't overmix the batter as
it will make the muffins heavy.

Divide the mixture evenly between the muffin
cases. I use an ice-cream scoop for this as it gives
a great uniformity to the muffins, making sure
that each one has the same quantity of mixture.

Mix the demerara sugar and desiccated coconut
together and scatter over each muffin for a lovely
crunchy topping.

Bake on the middle shelf of the preheated oven
for 30–35 minutes until the muffins are golden,
well risen and a skewer inserted into the middle
of the muffins comes out clean.

Cool slightly on a wire rack before serving.

Bits & Bobs

Herb teas
You can make really easy herb teas
using either one of those teapots with
the centre chamber that holds loose
leaves or in a cafetiere. Who needs
expensive mint tea when it's so
easy to make your own! See pages
248–9 for my favourite brews.

FRENCH-STYLE PANCAKES

I love pancakes and so do my boys: that's the thing with food, every dish either contains a memory or creates one. My cousin Ben and I always remember our Nanny Billie's pancakes; it's the association with someone you love that makes it a special dish. This isn't our nan's pancake recipe but the memory of the crêpe-style ones are all hers. When I make pancakes or Yorkshire puddings I use cups – not the measuring-type ones, just any old one I have in the cupboard.

1 mug of plain flour
**1 mug of full-fat or
  semi-skimmed milk**
3 large eggs
**a knob of unsalted
  butter, melted**
**sunflower oil for
  cooking pancakes**

To serve
caster sugar
lemon wedges
Nutella

Sift the flour into a mixing bowl and make a well in the middle. Whisk the milk, eggs and melted butter together in a jug and pour into the well in the flour. Using a balloon whisk, beat the mixture to make sure that all the flour is well incorporated and there are no lumps in the batter.

Heat a non-stick frying pan over a medium heat and add a teaspoon of oil to coat the base of the pan. Spoon a ladleful of batter into the pan, then swirl the pan so that the batter fills the bottom in an even layer. Cook for 30–40 seconds until set and the underside of the pancake is pale golden brown, then flip over, either with held breath and a quick flick of the wrist or, if you're nervous like me, with a fish slice.

Cook the other side for another 30 seconds or until golden brown.

Turn onto a plate and serve immediately with some freshly squeezed lemon juice and sugar or, if you're like my boys, a big dollop of Nutella.

Repeat with the remaining batter, adding more oil to the pan as needed.

AMERICAN PANCAKES

When I was a little girl we went on holiday to Florida and I had these incredibly fluffy pancakes. They stayed in my mind and so did the diner in which I had them, another foodie memory! Serve them with a juicy blueberry sauce - I promise you won't be disappointed.

3 large eggs, separated
1 mug of self-raising flour
1 mug of full-fat milk
a knob of unsalted butter, melted
a pinch of salt
sunflower oil for cooking the pancakes
unsalted butter for cooking the pancakes

Bits & Bobs

Sticky sauces
I think a sticky, sweet, fruity sauce with my pancakes is the way I'd like to start my day every Saturday! I love different textures, flavours and hot and cold combinations not just at breakfast time – they're great on ice cream too. See pages 248–9 for a couple of ideas that I'd like to share with you.

Whisk the egg whites in a clean, dry bowl until just stiff.

In another bowl mix together the flour, milk, egg yolks, melted butter and a pinch of salt.

Using a large metal spoon, fold the egg whites into the flour mixture, one third at a time.

Heat a tablespoon of oil and a little butter in a large non-stick frying pan over a medium heat; the butter gives the cooked pancakes a lovely nutty flavour.

Ladle 2–3 spoonfuls of batter into the pan, making 2–3 little pancakes (the batter will seem really thick, but this is how it should be).

Cook the pancakes for about 40 seconds, until the underside is golden and the little bubbles stop appearing on the top of the pancakes. Flip them over and cook the other side until golden brown and the pancakes have risen to about 1cm.

Remove from the pan and keep warm while you continue to cook more pancakes until you have used up all the batter, adding more oil to the pan as needed.

See pages 248–9 for a lovely blueberry sauce to serve your pancakes with.

DANISH PASTRY DOUGH

With Danish, you need to start the day before. It isn't a hard process, just really lengthy. All of the following Danish recipes use half this quantity of dough.

650g strong white flour,
** plus extra for kneading**
1 ½ tsp salt
7g fast-action/easy-blend yeast
85g caster sugar
425ml water, warm
500g unsalted butter, chilled

Flavoured glazes
I really love drizzling cakes and pastries with little glazes in different flavours. For ideas, see pages 248–9.

Tip the flour, salt, yeast and sugar into a large mixing bowl. Add the water and mix well until the dough comes together. Turn out onto a work surface and knead for five minutes until smooth.

Put the dough back into the clean bowl, cover with cling film and leave for 1 hour in a warm place or until doubled in size.

Meanwhile cut the butter into thick slices and arrange neatly in a rectangle on a large piece of baking parchment. Cover with another piece of parchment and, using a rolling pin, flatten the butter into a neat 20 x 40cm rectangle. Chill until needed.

Once the dough has doubled in size, turn it out onto a lightly floured work surface and knead again for 30 seconds to knock it back. Roll the dough out into a 20 x 60cm rectangle, roughly 1cm thick and with the short (20cm) edge nearest to you.

Peel the top sheet of parchment off the butter and lay it butter-side down on the top two-thirds of the dough rectangle. Peel off the top sheet of parchment from the butter. Fold the bottom unbuttered third of the dough up onto the butter to cover it halfway.

Fold down the buttered top third of the dough over this to cover neatly. You should now have a square of dough roughly one-third of the size of the rectangle that you started with. Turn the dough 90 degrees clockwise and roll it out again into a neat rectangle roughly 1cm thick. Fold the top third of the dough down to the middle and the bottom third up over this. Turn the dough 90 degrees again, cover with cling film and place in fridge to rest for 1 hour. Repeat this rolling and folding process another four times. Leave in fridge overnight.

PAIN AU CHOCOLAT

These are so simple once you've made the dough: as long as you remember to place them on the baking tray seam-side down and use only chocolate that you'd want to eat, you really can't go wrong.

plain flour for rolling out
½ quantity of Danish
pastry dough
10 squares of chocolate
1 egg, beaten with 1 tbsp water
3 tbsp apricot jam, warmed
and sieved

You will need two baking trays
covered with baking parchment

Lightly dust the work surface with plain flour and roll the dough into a large rectangle roughly 1cm thick.

Cut the dough into 8–10 equal-size strips, each strip roughly 15–18cm long and 7–9cm wide.

Place a chunk of your favourite chocolate onto one end of each strip and lightly brush a little egg wash on the other end. Roll the dough from the chocolate end towards you so that the chocolate is in the middle of each pastry.

Arrange the pastries on two parchment-lined baking trays, making sure that the seam is underneath. Cover loosely with cling film and leave to rise for 45 minutes.

Preheat the oven to 220°C/425°F/Gas Mark 7.

Brush the top of each pastry with egg wash.

Bake the pain au chocolat, one tray at a time, on the middle shelf of the preheated oven for 15–18 minutes until golden brown.

Brush with a little warmed, sieved apricot jam.

PECAN SWIRLS

I think anything with pecan and maple syrup is a winner: the warming, comforting flavour is so wonderfully earthy. When I came up with this idea I couldn't wait to try it out and I wasn't disappointed.

200g pecans, chopped
175g demerara sugar
2 tsp ground cinnamon
plain flour for rolling out
½ quantity Danish pastry dough
40g unsalted butter, melted
1 egg, beaten with 1 tbsp water
2–3 tbsp maple syrup, warmed

You will need two baking trays covered with baking parchment

Mix the chopped pecans, sugar and cinnamon in a bowl.

Lightly dust the work surface with plain flour and roll the dough out into a neat rectangle roughly 1cm thick and with the long side closest to you.

Brush the top of the dough liberally with melted butter and scatter over the nut mixture in an even layer.

Starting with the edge closest to you, roll the dough into a tight spiral, neatly encasing the nut mixture.

Slice the roll into 5cm lengths and place cut side uppermost on parchment-covered baking trays. Using the palm of your hand, flatten each pastry slightly, cover with cling film and leave in a warm place for about 1 hour.

Preheat the oven to 200°C/400°F/Gas Mark 6.

Brush the top of each pastry with the egg wash and bake on the middle shelf of the preheated oven for about 15 minutes until golden brown.

Remove from the oven and brush the top of each pastry with a little warmed maple syrup.

COCONUT AND CRANBERRY DANISH

I had all my girlfriends over for brunch the first time I made this and they couldn't eat it quickly enough.

100g dried cranberries
300g full-fat cream cheese
80g desiccated coconut
50g caster sugar
zest of 1 orange, grated
plain flour for rolling out
1 egg, beaten with 1 tbsp water
10–12 sugar cubes, crushed

You will need a large baking tray covered with baking parchment

Combine the cranberries, cream cheese, coconut, caster sugar and orange zest in a mixing bowl.

Lightly dust the work surface with plain flour. Roll the dough into a neat 40 x 20cm rectangle and trim the edges. Place the dough on the baking tray and turn the rectangle so that the long side is closest to you.

Spoon the filling in a neat line vertically down the centre third of the dough leaving a 3–4cm border at the top and bottom.

Starting on the right-hand side, cut the dough into downward diagonal strips roughly 2–3cm wide to create a 'fringe' on one side of the filling. Repeat this on the left-hand side. Fold the top and bottom edges of the dough over onto the filling.

Starting at the top right-hand side, fold one piece of dough fringe up and over the filling. Fold over a piece of dough from the opposite side in a plaiting motion. Repeat until you reach the bottom.

Cover loosely with cling film and leave to prove for 40–60 minutes.

Preheat the oven to 200°C/400°F/Gas Mark 6.

Brush the pastry with the beaten egg and sprinkle with crushed sugar cubes.

Bake on the middle shelf of the oven for 30–40 minutes or until golden.

Serve warm or at room temperature.

CROISSANTS

*24 years ago I was lucky enough to have a holiday in Rio de Janeiro.
I can't remember the name of the hotel we stayed in but I can remember
the pastry chef who produced the best croissants I've ever tasted!*

**½ quantity of Danish
pastry dough**

Bits & Bobs

Easy Strawberry Jam
There's nothing like making your
own jam to serve on home-made
scones or fresh-baked crumpets.
See pages 248–9 for a simplified
version to get you started.

On a lightly floured work surface roll the
dough into a rectangle roughly 1cm thick.

Cut into 12 equal triangles.

Roll from wider end into crescents.

Place on a baking tray with the pointy end
on the tray.

Leave for 40–60 minutes to double in size.

Brush with egg wash.

Bake for 22 minutes or until golden brown.

Place on a wire rack to cool.

Brush with some warmed, sieved apricot jam.

PORRIDGE WITH STICKY BANANA

I think porridge is a nutritious breakfast and it can almost keep you going for the whole day. I always find half a cup of porridge oats to a cup of milk per person is about right. I've got to admit I nuke mine in the microwave for about 4-5 minutes, then cover with a piece of kitchen roll and leave it to stand for the same amount of time. Stir and it's perfectly creamy porridge.

a knob of unsalted butter
1 heaped tbsp brown sugar
1 small firm banana

Melt the butter and brown sugar in a frying pan over a medium heat.

Slice the banana, add to the pan and cook for 3-4 minutes until tender, caramelized and sticky.

Spoon the porridge into a bowl and top with the cooked banana and any pan juices.

SINGING HINNIES

I'd never tried these before writing my book, but I know these will be a firm favourite in our house from now on.

250g self-raising flour
a pinch of salt
60g unsalted butter,
    chilled and diced
60g lard, chilled and diced,
    plus extra for greasing
90g currants
1 large egg, beaten
2–3 tbsp full-fat milk
    to combine
plain flour for rolling out

To serve
butter
clotted cream
honey
jam

You will also need
a 6cm round cutter

Sift the flour and salt into a bowl. Add the diced butter and lard, and using your fingers rub into the flour until thoroughly combined and the mixture looks like crumble or sand.

Add the currants, beaten egg and enough milk to combine and to bring the dough together.

Lightly dust the work surface with plain flour and roll out the dough to a thickness of about 5 mm.

Using a plain cutter, stamp out 6cm circles from the dough. Re-roll and stamp out the offcuts until you have used up all the dough.

Heat a heavy-based frying pan over a medium heat and lightly grease the pan with a little lard.

Add the singing hinnies to the pan and cook for about 3 minutes on each side until golden, turning down the heat if they are browning too quickly.

Serve warm with butter, clotted cream, honey, jam or a combination of whatever takes your fancy.

BAKED OMELETTE

The idea of something that you can prep, pop into the oven and forget about for a while is appealing to me because it gives me time to get on with other things. If you're anything like me you may need a timer, as I sometimes forget what's cooking and that's not so good.

2 tbsp olive oil
6 rashers of streaky
   bacon, diced
2 shallots, peeled and
   finely chopped
a pinch of chopped fresh
   rosemary (use dried
   if you don't have fresh)
6 large eggs
100g cheddar cheese, grated
50ml double cream
30g unsalted butter, melted
salt and freshly ground
   black pepper

Preheat the oven to 190°C/375°F/Gas Mark 5.

Heat half of the olive oil in a frying pan, add the chopped bacon, shallots and rosemary, and cook until the onions are tender and the bacon is nicely browned at the edges.

Wipe out the pan.

In a large open-necked jug, whisk together the eggs, cheese, cream and melted butter. Add the bacon mixture to the jug, season and stir to combine thoroughly.

Heat the remaining oil in the frying pan over a medium heat. Add the egg mixture and slide the pan into the preheated oven. Bake for about 20 minutes or until just set and golden brown. Remove from the oven and leave to settle for 5 minutes before cutting into wedges to serve.

APPLE AND CINNAMON WAFFLES

For waffles it is almost the same as American pancake batter. I've just bought a new electric waffle iron and am always trying out new ideas with it.

3 large or 4 medium eggs
1 mug of self-raising flour
1 mug of full-fat milk
70g unsalted butter, melted
1 ½ tsp ground cinnamon
2 eating apples, coarsely grated

To serve
25g butter

Preheat the waffle iron.

Start by separating the eggs into 2 mixing bowls. Whisk the egg whites until they reach soft peaks.

In the other bowl combine the egg yolks, flour, milk, melted butter and cinnamon.

Put the grated apple into a clean tea towel, twist to squeeze out the excess juice and add the apple to the batter. Using a large metal spoon, fold the egg whites one third at a time into the batter, making sure to combine well or you'll end up with pockets of egg white in your waffles.

Spoon the batter into a waffle iron and cook until golden. Remove and keep warm while you repeat until all the batter has been used up.

Serve the warm waffles with some butter, whipped with an electric whisk until pale and fluffy.

Chapter two

BRUNCH

*For me, brunch is a very social occasion: by 11 a.m.,
I'm happy to have the hustle and bustle of a room
full to the brim with people chatting around a
scrubbed pine table groaning with food, hot coffee
pots, glass jugs of juices and some tasty delights
to fill your tummy and your soul.*

♥

PIGGIES IN BLANKETS DANISH

These are wonderful and I think that for people who love Danish but haven't got a particularly sweet tooth this is the very thing. Gorgeous light flaky pastry with that fresh, cutting tomato flavour topped with a wonderful sausage wrapped in bacon.

½ **quantity of Danish pastry dough, see page 20**
plain flour for rolling out
10 rashers of streaky bacon
10 chipolatas
1 tbsp sunflower or light olive oil
6 tbsp tomato chutney or home-made tomato sauce
1 egg, beaten with 1 tbsp water

You will also need
2 baking trays

Lightly dust the work surface with plain flour and roll out the dough into a rectangle.

Cut the dough into neat 12–15cm squares. Fold two opposite corners of each square to meet in the middle.

Arrange the pastries on two baking trays, cover loosely with cling film and leave to prove for 1 hour.

Preheat the oven to 200°C/400°F/Gas Mark 6.

Meanwhile, wrap a rasher of bacon around each chipolata, heat a tablespoon of oil in a frying pan and flash fry a few sausages at a time until just starting to brown. Remove from the pan and drain on kitchen paper to remove excess oil.

Spoon the chutney or tomato sauce into a small saucepan and reduce over a low heat until you have a thick paste, stirring with a wooden spoon to prevent the sauce catching on the bottom of the pan.

Brush the pastries with a little egg wash, then top with a spoonful of chutney and a bacon-wrapped sausage, seam side down.

Cook on the middle shelf of the preheated oven for about 25 minutes until golden brown. Serve warm.

OVEN-BAKED BREAKFAST

This is a lovely easy weekend brunch for when I'm not ready for a big breakfast but then too hungry to wait until lunchtime.

For every person I'd suggest:
1 good-quality sausage
a handful of button mushrooms
a knob of butter
1 tomato
olive oil
a pinch of fresh thyme leaves
2 rashers of good-quality bacon
1 egg
salt and freshly ground black
   pepper

You will need 1 baking tray for every 2 people eating

Bits
& Bobs

Eggy Bread
Sometimes you may feel a little peckish but there isn't much in the cupboard apart from perhaps an egg and a slice of white bread that's past its best. Don't despair: if a look in the spice rack then reveals some cinnamon, you've got more than enough for an excellent gap-filler.
See pages 248–9.

Preheat the oven to 220°C/425°F/Gas Mark 7.

Pop the baking tray into the oven to heat up for a couple of minutes.

Prick the sausages with a fork and put onto the hot baking tray. Turn the oven down to 200°C/400°F/Gas Mark 6 and cook for 4 minutes.

Slice the mushrooms and arrange in a pile in one corner of the baking tray, top with a knob of butter and season with a pinch of salt and freshly ground black pepper. Return to the oven and continue to bake for another 6 minutes.

Cut the tomato in half, brush with olive oil, scatter with thyme, season and place onto the baking tray along with the bacon rashers.

Cook for a further 8–10 minutes until the bacon is nice and crisp.

Transfer everything onto a heated plate, cover with foil and keep warm. Break one egg per person directly onto the hot baking tray, return to the oven and cook for about 2 minutes until set and cooked to your liking.

Serve with a big pot of tea and some toasted sliced bloomer.

BLACKCURRANT AND CREAM CHEESE PANCAKES

How fantastic is the colour of blackcurrants, especially when they pop while cooking and that gorgeous purple shows through. Use a regular coffee cup or a smallish glass – as long as you use the same vessel to measure all the ingredients it will be fine.

1 cup of self-raising flour
1 tsp baking powder
1 cup of full-fat milk and full-fat cream cheese combined – roughly half-and-half
1 tsp vanilla extract
3 large eggs
a knob of unsalted butter, melted
½ cup of fresh blackcurrants
sunflower oil to cook

To serve, optional
unsalted butter
caster sugar

Combine the flour, baking powder, milk and cream cheese, vanilla, eggs and melted butter in a large bowl. Whisk until smooth and thoroughly combined. Add the blackcurrants and fold in using a large metal spoon.

Heat a couple of tablespoons of oil in a large frying pan over a medium heat. Using a large spoon, drop three spoonfuls of batter into the pan to make 3 pancakes.

Cook for about 40 seconds until the bubbles have stopped appearing on the top of the pancake and the underside is golden. Flip the pancakes over and cook the other side until golden brown.

Remove from the pan and keep warm. Continue to cook more in the same way until all the batter has been used up, adding more oil to the pan as needed.

Serve with a little butter and sugar if desired.

CINNAMON AND SUGAR POPOVERS

Children will love these: they are almost like those doughnuts that you buy at the seafront but without the deep-fat frying. You can buy the special tins really easily online or for slightly smaller popovers just use the deepest muffin tin you can find. I use cups: just any coffee cup you have in the cupboard will do.

1 cup of plain flour
1 cup of full-fat milk
3 large eggs, beaten
½ tsp vanilla extract
½ tsp almond extract
1 tbsp caster sugar
a pinch of salt
a knob of unsalted
    butter, melted
3 tbsp sunflower oil

To serve
75g unsalted butter, melted
3 tbsp caster sugar
3 tbsp ground cinnamon

You will need a 12-hole muffin or popover tin

Preheat the oven to 200°C/400°F/Gas Mark 6.

Tip all the ingredients apart from the sunflower oil into a large mixing bowl and beat until smooth with a balloon whisk. Pour the batter into a large jug.

Pour 1–2 teaspoons of sunflower oil into each hole of the popover or muffin tin and heat in the oven for 5 minutes.

Remove the tin from the oven – be careful as the oil will be hot. Pour the batter into the tin: it should come halfway up each hole and will sizzle slightly in the hot oil.

Bake on the middle shelf of the preheated oven for about 30 minutes or until the popovers are very well risen and golden brown.

Remove from the tins and brush each popover with melted butter.

Combine the sugar and ground cinnamon in a bowl and roll the hot popovers in the mixture to coat completely.

Serve warm or at room temperature and on the day of baking.

CHURROS

*I have fond memories of churros as a young girl. My schoolfriend
Jayne's dad was Spanish, and he used to make them for us
whenever I stayed over at their place.*

150ml full-fat milk
1 tsp lemon juice
60g unsalted butter, diced
80g plain flour
a pinch of salt
2 large eggs, beaten
1 litre sunflower oil for
   deep frying (fresh)
caster sugar
ground cinnamon

Dipping sauce
100g dark chocolate, chopped
100ml double cream

You will need a piping bag
fitted with a large star nozzle

Warm the milk, lemon juice and butter in a saucepan over a gentle heat to melt the butter. The mixture may curdle slightly but this doesn't matter. Quickly bring the mixture to a rolling boil, then immediately remove the pan from the heat and sift in the flour and salt. Beat quickly with a wooden spoon until smooth and the mixture leaves the side of the pan. Leave to one side to cool slightly until the mixture is warm to the touch.

Gradually mix in the eggs, beating with a wooden spoon until the batter is smooth and shiny.

Heat the oil in a heavy-based saucepan over a medium heat – to test the temperature, add a small piece of bread to the hot oil and it should sizzle and turn golden in 20 seconds.

Spoon the mixture into a piping bag fitted with a large star nozzle. Hold the piping bag in one hand and pipe 8–10cm lengths of batter directly into the hot oil. Using a pair of scissors in your other hand, snip the batter away from the nozzle. Cook only 3–4 churros at a time as you don't want to crowd the pan and lower the temperature of the hot oil.

Cook for 2–3 minutes until puffed and golden brown, remove from the pan with a slotted spoon and drain on kitchen paper. Sprinkle the churros with a mixture of caster sugar and ground cinnamon. Repeat until you have used up all the batter.

Heat the chopped chocolate and double cream in a small saucepan over a low heat until the chocolate has melted. Stir until smooth for a lovely dipping sauce.

CRUMPETS

Roaring fires, big mugs of hot chocolate, the Sunday papers and home-made crumpets… total bliss is the only way to describe that.

500g strong bread flour
1 tsp salt
2 tsp caster sugar
7g easy-blend/fast-action yeast
250ml water, warmed
350ml full-fat milk, warmed
oil for greasing

You will also need a flat griddle pan or solid-based, non-stick frying pan and 4 x 7–8cm crumpet rings or plain cutters

In a large bowl combine the flour, salt, sugar and yeast and make a well in the centre.

Mix together the warm water and milk in a jug and whisk into the flour to make a thick, smooth batter. Cover with a clean tea towel and leave to rise for about 1 hour.

Heat a flat griddle pan or non-stick frying pan over a very low heat and spray or brush with a little oil. Add the crumpet rings or pastry cutters and pour the batter into the rings, filling each one to just under two-thirds full. Cook over a very low heat until the bottom of the crumpet is golden brown, the top is covered in bubble holes and the batter appears dry. This can take up to 10 minutes.

Remove the rings, flip the crumpets over and cook on the other side for about 90 seconds until tinged with brown.

Repeat until all of the batter has been used up.

BREAKFAST QUICHE

All the flavours of breakfast in a quiche, just perfect for brunch.
Serve with some salad leaves, crusty bread and lots of time
to relax and enjoy it.

1 quantity of shortcrust
  pastry (see page 200)

Filling
10–20g butter
2 tbsp light olive oil
100g button mushrooms,
  sliced into 3
240g good-quality bacon
  rashers
400ml double cream
a splash of lemon juice
4 large eggs
50g cheddar, grated
freshly ground black pepper

You will need a 21–23cm
loose-bottomed tart tin

Bits
& Bobs

Home-made tomato sauce
A little home-made tomato sauce
with my baked omelette or breakfast
quiche makes it just a little extra
special. See pages 248–9 for a
quick and easy method.

Dust the work surface with flour and roll the pastry
out to a thickness of 2–3 mm. Carefully line the tart
tin with the pastry, trim off any excess and prick
the base with a fork. Chill for 20 minutes while you
preheat the oven to 200°C/400°F/Gas Mark 6.

Line the tart shell with baking parchment and
baking beans and place on a baking tray. Bake
for 20 minutes and then remove the beans and
parchment and bake for a further 5–10 minutes
until pale golden.

Turn the oven down to 160°C/320°F/Gas Mark 3.

Heat the butter and 1 tablespoon of olive oil in a
frying pan, add the sliced mushrooms and gently
sauté until tender and all of the mushroomy juice
has evaporated. Remove from the pan and put
to one side. Chop each of the bacon rashers into
three pieces and heat 1 tablespoon of olive oil
in the frying pan. Add the bacon and cook over
a medium heat until crisp and golden.

Beat the cream, lemon juice, eggs and cheese
in a bowl until thoroughly combined.

Spread the bacon and mushrooms in an even
layer in the bottom of the cooked pastry case.
Pour in the cream mixture and bake the quiche
for 35 minutes or until just wobbly in the centre.

Remove from the oven and leave the quiche
to stand and firm up in the tin for 10 minutes
before serving.

ENGLISH MUFFINS

I always remember the English muffins I had as a child. They came from Marks & Spencer and we ate them toasted with jam and butter. In later life I started to make them myself, and found that they work perfectly as a brunch item with eggs Benedict. I know this recipe is not easy, but I believe that it is well worth the effort.

**450g strong bread flour,
    plus extra for kneading**
7g easy-blend/fast-action yeast
1 tsp salt
1 tsp caster sugar
300ml full-fat milk
fine cornmeal/polenta to dust
lard for cooking muffins

You will also need a 6.5cm plain round cutter and a flat griddle pan

Mix the flour, yeast, salt and sugar in the bowl of a free-standing mixer and make a well in the centre.

Warm the milk until hand-hot, pour into the dry ingredients and mix to combine. Knead for about 8 minutes until the dough is smooth and elastic. Shape the dough into a ball and place in a large, oiled bowl. Cover with cling film and leave in a warm place for about 1 hour or until doubled in size.

Turn the dough out of the bowl onto a lightly floured work surface and knead by hand for a couple of minutes to knock back the dough. Return the dough to the bowl, cover and set aside for another 25 minutes.

On a lightly floured work surface, roll out the dough to a thickness of 2cm and cut out 10 muffins using a plain round 6½cm cutter. Arrange on a baking tray, sprinkle with cornmeal/polenta and leave to prove for 30 minutes.

Heat a flat griddle or heavy-based frying pan over a medium heat and brush with a little lard. Cook the muffins in batches on the hot griddle pan for about 7 minutes on each side until well risen and golden.

Split the muffins in half through the middle and griddle on the cut side for about a minute more and serve immediately.

BLUEBERRY MUFFIN LOAF

The idea of this fruity loaf to share at brunch is that it will retain its moisture; a whole loaf of loveliness, sweet plump blueberries, crispy crunchy topping and light airy sponge. It's not just a single sensation but all different flavours and textures, a little party on your tongue.

Topping
25g plain flour
20g unsalted butter, diced
20g caster sugar

Muffin
200g self-raising flour
½ tsp bicarbonate of soda
75g soft brown sugar
50g caster sugar
70g unsalted butter, melted
160ml full-fat milk
1 large egg
1 tsp vanilla extract
130g blueberries

You will need a greased 900g (2lb) loaf tin, the base and ends lined with a strip of buttered baking parchment

Preheat oven 180°C/350°F/Gas Mark 4.

Make the topping first. Tip the flour, butter and sugar into a bowl and, using your fingers, rub the butter into the flour until it resembles a crumble mixture.

To make the loaf, sieve the flour and bicarbonate of soda into a bowl, add both of the sugars and mix well.

Melt the butter, leave to cool slightly and then mix with the milk, egg and vanilla extract and whisk until smooth.

Make a well in the centre of the dry ingredients and pour in the milk and egg mixture. Using a large metal spoon, fold the two mixtures together until only just combined. Fold the blueberries into the mixture, making sure not to overwork the batter as this will result in a heavy sponge.

Carefully spoon the mixture into the prepared loaf tin, scatter over the crumble topping and bake on the middle shelf of the preheated oven for about 1 hour or until golden, well risen and a skewer inserted into the middle of the cake comes out clean.

Serve warm or at room temperature.

Bits & Bobs

Fruit smoothies
A big jug of fruit smoothie is a wonderful addition to any brunch table, a perfect way to get at least 3 of your 5 a day. I make smoothies often and what's even better is that children don't realise they are drinking so much goodness! See pages 248–9 for my favourite combinations.

Chapter three

FAMILY BAKING

How nice to have family favourites: it's like creating your own history, something you can pass down from generation to generation, each one with a memory, maybe of a happy Sunday tea when your youngest took his first step, or a sunny afternoon with a group of women whom twenty-five years later you are still honoured to call your friends, or the lovely moist fruity loaf that reminds you of a much loved auntie.

RASPBERRY TORTE

I've been baking this torte for the last twenty-five years: it never disappoints and it's so simple, requiring all the same weights of ingredients, a quick whisk and a pop into the oven. I'm forever grateful to my lovely friend Linda for this recipe.

150g self-raising flour
150g unsalted butter, softened
150g caster sugar
150g ground almonds
2 large eggs, beaten
150g fresh raspberries,
   plus extra to serve
icing sugar to dust

You will also need a 23cm cake tin, buttered and the base lined with a disc of buttered baking parchment

Preheat the oven to 180°C/350°F/Gas Mark 4.

Tip the flour, soft butter, sugar, ground almonds and eggs into a bowl and beat together until pale, light and fluffy.

Spoon the cake mixture into the prepared tin and spread level with a palette knife. Push the raspberries, pointy sides up, into the batter.

Bake on the middle shelf of the preheated oven for about 1 hour, checking the cake after 45 minutes and covering it loosely with foil once it has browned to prevent the top colouring too much.

Cool in the tin for 5 minutes and then transfer the torte to a cooling rack until cold. Scatter with extra raspberries and dust with icing sugar to serve.

VICTORIA SANDWICH

I love Victoria sandwich cake: it reminds me of all things British – Sunday tea, the Women's Institute, family parties – and you're never more than one step away from making one, as all of the ingredients are normally in the store cupboard. I serve mine just with jam, but you could add buttercream if you like.

Cake
200g self-raising flour
1 tsp baking powder
200g caster sugar
200g margarine,
    at room temperature
4 large eggs, beaten
1 large egg yolk
1 tsp vanilla extract
    or vanilla bean paste

Filling
4 tbsp strawberry jam
2 tbsp caster sugar

You will need two 20cm sandwich tins

Bits & Bobs

Buttercream
With all baking I think it's about the individual's own taste, but I have developed my own buttercream over the years which I like best. You can add anything from butterscotch to orange juice to suit whatever kind of cake you are icing. See pages 248–9 for my recipe and flavour suggestions.

Preheat the oven to 180°C/350°F/Gas Mark 4. Butter and line the base of each cake tin with a disc of buttered baking parchment.

Tip all of the cake ingredients into the bowl of a free-standing mixer and beat for 2 minutes until smooth. If you don't have a free-standing mixer, you can use an electric hand-held mixer.

Divide the batter evenly between the prepared cake tins and spread level using a palette knife. Bake on the middle shelf of the preheated oven for about 25–30 minutes or until golden, well risen and a skewer inserted into the middle of the cakes comes out clean.

Remove from the oven and carefully turn the cakes out of the tins, peel off the parchment and leave to cool on wire cooling racks.

Place one of the cold cakes on a serving plate, right side up, and spread with jam (and buttercream if using). Top with the second cake and sprinkle with caster sugar to serve.

Family baking

CHOCOLATE MUD CAKE

This is such a well-behaved sponge: I make it really often, it's so simple and normally I have all the ingredients in the cupboard and fridge (if you don't have sour cream, use double cream with 2 teaspoons of lemon juice). I never really liked chocolate cake before this one and, to be honest, I'm still not a lover of the artificial-tasting, shop-bought ones, but this moist chocolate cake is so good – I haven't found anyone who doesn't like it.

175g unsalted butter, softened
300g caster sugar
3 large eggs, beaten
75g self-raising flour
200g plain flour
1 tsp bicarbonate of soda
75g cocoa
200ml sour cream, at room temperature
50g full-fat cream cheese, at room temperature

You will need a 20cm round spring form or cake tin, buttered and the base lined with a disc of buttered baking parchment

Preheat the oven to 180°C/350°F/Gas Mark 4.

Beat the butter and caster sugar together until pale, light and fluffy: this is easiest using either a free-standing or an electric hand-held mixer.

Gradually add the beaten eggs a little at a time, beating well between each addition.

Sift both of the flours, bicarbonate of soda and the cocoa into a bowl. Add half of the sifted dry ingredients to the egg and sugar mixture and fold in using a large metal spoon.

In another bowl, mix the sour cream and cream cheese together until smooth. Add half to the cake batter and fold in.

Repeat this process with the remaining flour and sour cream and mix until smooth.

Spoon the cake batter into the prepared tin and spread level with a palette knife. Bake on the middle shelf of the preheated oven for about 1 hour or until a wooden skewer inserted into the middle of the cake comes out clean.

Leave the cake to cool in the tin for 10 minutes before turning out onto a wire rack.

Cover the cake with a buttercream flavoured with syrup, liqueur or a chocolate ganache (see pages 248–9).

Bits & Bobs

Flavoured syrups
Flavoured syrups are fantastic for adding extra taste and moisture into a bake by brushing the top of the cake when it comes out of the oven. You can make a basic chocolate syrup for topping a mud cake, or be adventurous and go for a rosemary and thyme glaze! See pages 248–9 for recipes.

Family baking

WHITE CHOCOLATE TIFFIN

My friend Di loves tiffin so I set about making her one from white chocolate: I'm pleased to say she loved it.

250g digestive biscuits
60g shredded, dried or
    desiccated coconut
60g glacé cherries, washed,
    dried and halved
125g unsalted butter
2 tbsp golden syrup
2 tbsp malted drink powder
    (such as Horlicks or Ovaltine)
1 tbsp caster sugar
500g white chocolate

**You will need a 30 x 23cm
baking tin with a depth of
about 4cm. Lightly grease
the tin and line with a sheet
of baking parchment**

Tip the digestive biscuits into a freezer bag and, using a rolling pin, crush them into smallish, random-sized pieces and tip into a bowl. Add the coconut and cherries.

Tip the butter, golden syrup, malted drink powder and sugar into a small saucepan. Place over a low heat and stir constantly until the butter has melted and the mixture is thoroughly combined. Pour into the bowl over the crushed biscuits and stir until evenly coated.

Spoon the mixture into the prepared tin and press into an even layer. Leave until completely cold.

Break the white chocolate into chunks and melt in a heatproof bowl either over a pan of barely simmering water or gently in the microwave, in short bursts and on a low setting. Stir until smooth, spread over the tiffin base and leave until set completely.

Cut the tiffin into squares using a knife that you have run under hot water to warm the blade: this makes it easier and neater to cut through the chocolate.

BLACKBERRY AND APPLE LOAF CAKE

I love blackberries: they remind me of the time of year when my son Dylan was born, late September when all the summer fruits are coming to an end and then these gorgeous purple gems appear. For me, a classic blackberry and apple cake is always going to be a winner.

Topping
60g unsalted butter,
    chilled and diced
80g plain flour
2 heaped tbsp demerara sugar

Cake
170g self-raising flour
170g unsalted butter, softened
170g caster sugar
3 large eggs, beaten
170g (prepared weight) apples
    such as Braeburns or Cox's,
    peeled, cored and diced
70g blackberries

You will also need a 900g (2lb) loaf tin, the inside buttered and the base and ends lined with a strip of buttered baking parchment

Preheat the oven to 180°C/350°F/Gas Mark 4.

Combine the topping ingredients: rub the butter into the flour and sugar either in a food processor using the pulse button or with your hands. Once the mixture reaches a crumble-type consistency, put it to one side while you make the cake batter.

Tip the flour, butter, sugar and eggs into a bowl and, either using a free-standing mixer or an electric hand whisk, beat until really light and creamy. Gently fold in the diced apples and blackberries using a large metal spoon.

Spoon the cake mixture into the prepared tin, spread level and sprinkle over the crumble topping in an even layer.

Bake on the middle shelf of the preheated oven for about 1 hour or until a skewer inserted into the middle of the cake comes away cleanly.

Cool the cake in the tin for about 5 minutes and then carefully lift it out onto a wire rack to cool completely.

BREAD PUDDING

My dad's family were tightly knit: there were eight brothers and sisters, and every Saturday all the aunties used to pop into my nanny Jess's house with all the cousins. There was always a lovely bake from one of them, and bread pudding still really reminds me of my Auntie Carol. I've been baking it since I've had my own family and it's now Billy's firm favourite.

1 x 400g loaf of two-day-old
   white bread (crusts on)
550ml full-fat milk
300g mixed dried fruit
1 tbsp mixed peel paste
   (see below)
1 large egg, beaten
100g suet or unsalted
   butter, melted
5 tsp ground mixed spice
100g soft light brown sugar

To serve
4 tbsp caster sugar

**You will also need a greased
20 x 25cm ovenproof dish or tin**

Preheat the oven to 180°C/350°F/Gas Mark 4.

Break the bread into 4cm chunks and tip into a large mixing bowl. Pour over the milk, mix well and leave to soak for 30 minutes.

Add the remaining ingredients and mix well to combine thoroughly. Spoon the mixture into the prepared dish in an even layer and bake on the middle shelf of the preheated oven for about 45–50 minutes or until golden brown and set.

Leave the bread pudding to cool before sprinkling with caster sugar and cutting into thick slices to serve.

Bits
& Bobs

Mixed peel paste
I really like the flavour of mixed peel in my baking but I can't stand the texture of those pieces of peel. So for years I have been processing mine to a paste, resulting in all the lovely taste and none of the pieces. See pages 248–9.

APPLE AND HAZELNUT STREUSEL CAKE

*I love different toppings: they give my cakes an extra dimension,
a different texture. This one adds a lovely toasty, nutty flavour.*

100g blanched hazelnuts
125g unsalted butter, softened
125g light muscovado sugar
2 large eggs, beaten
225g self-raising flour
1 tsp baking powder
1 tsp ground mixed spice
500g (prepared weight) apples
    such as Braeburns or Cox's,
    peeled, cored and diced
3 tbsp full-fat milk

Streusel
40g blanched hazelnuts
40g plain flour
25g dark brown sugar
25g unsalted butter, diced

**You will also need a 23cm
cake tin, greased and the base
lined with a disc of buttered
baking parchment**

Preheat the oven to 180°C/350°F/Gas Mark 4.

Tip the hazelnuts for both the cake and the streusel into a small roasting tin and lightly toast in the oven for 5 minutes until pale golden – set a timer so that you don't forget them! Chop the nuts and leave to cool.

Prepare the streusel before you make the cake batter. Tip 40g of the chopped, toasted hazelnuts, the flour, sugar and butter into a processor and blend until crumbly. You can also do this by hand: rub the butter into the flour, add the sugar and chopped nuts and mix to combine.

To make the cake, cream the softened butter and muscovado sugar until light and fluffy. Gradually add the beaten eggs, mixing well between each addition.

Sift in the flour, baking powder and mixed spice and mix lightly. Add the diced apples, the remaining chopped hazelnuts and the milk. Mix until smooth and thoroughly combined.

Spoon the cake mixture into the prepared tin and spread level.

Scatter the streusel evenly over the top of the cake and bake on the middle shelf of the preheated oven for about 50 minutes to 1 hour. The cake is cooked when it is golden brown and a wooden skewer comes out cleanly when tested in the middle of the cake.

BRAZIL NUT BROWNIES

My middle son, Jesse, has always loved chocolate with nuts, particularly in brownies, and I suddenly got an urge to create something similar that he would like even more. This is what I came up with. It's even moister and chewier than the original – good enough to eat at any time of the year, not just during the traditional Christmas festivities.

100g dark chocolate, chopped
85g milk chocolate, chopped
115g unsalted butter, diced
300g caster sugar
1 tsp vanilla extract or
  bean paste
2 large eggs, beaten
100g plain flour
50g self-raising flour
30g cocoa powder
80g Brazil nuts, chopped

You will also need a 20cm square baking tin, greased and lined with baking parchment

Preheat the oven to 170°C/325°F/Gas Mark 3.

Tip the dark chocolate and 25g of the milk chocolate into a heatproof bowl. Add the butter and melt together, either in the microwave on a low setting or in the bowl set over a saucepan of barely simmering water. Stir until smooth and leave to cool slightly.

Add the sugar, vanilla and beaten eggs to the melted chocolate and butter, and mix to combine. Sift both of the flours and cocoa powder into the bowl and mix until smooth.

Fold in the chopped Brazil nuts and the remaining 60g of chopped milk chocolate. Spoon into the prepared tin, spread level and bake on the middle shelf of the preheated oven for 30–35 minutes.

Leave to cool in the tin, then cut into squares and serve either as a cake or as a dessert with ice cream.

LEMON DRIZZLE TRAYBAKE

I love traybakes: they remind me of the wonderful Mary Berry, to whom I owe my knowledge of AGA cooking and baking. When we moved into our home, I inherited the AGA with the house and, to be honest, after the first excitement wore off, I realized that with no temperature control on the appliance I needed to learn quickly, so I went and bought a couple of Mary's AGA books. The rest, as they say, is history.

300g unsalted butter, softened
340g caster sugar
5 large eggs, beaten
340g self-raising flour
50ml full-fat milk
finely grated zest and juice
  of 2 lemons
150g granulated sugar

You will also need a 25 x 20cm tin, greased and lined with baking parchment

Bits & Bobs

Lemon and Marscapone cream
For a fresh creamy topping for your traybake, see pages 248–9 for a quick and easy recipe.

Preheat the oven to 180°C/350°F/Gas Mark 4.

Cream the butter and caster sugar together until pale, light and fluffy: this is easiest in a free-standing mixer or by using an electric hand whisk. Gradually add the beaten eggs, mixing well between each addition. Sift in the flour and mix to combine. Add the milk and grated lemon zest and mix again until smooth.

Spoon the mixture into the prepared tin and spread level using a palette knife.

Bake on the middle shelf of the preheated oven for about 1 hour, or until well risen, golden and a wooden skewer inserted into the middle of the cake comes out clean.

Remove the cake from the oven. Mix the lemon juice with the granulated sugar and slowly pour over the top. Leave the cake to cool in the tin before serving.

CARROT CAKE TRAYBAKE

This lovely moist traybake is always a sure thing for me: I've been making it for years and years. If you cook it for a children's party, you may well find that the visitors' parents stay to make sure they get some of it themselves! When cut in larger slices, it also makes a great family dessert.

Cake
300g soft light brown sugar
250ml sunflower oil
3 large eggs
150g self-raising flour
2 tsp ground mixed spice
a pinch of salt
250g carrots, coarsely grated
125g pecans, chopped
zest of half an orange,
    finely grated

Orange syrup
juice of half a large orange
20g caster sugar

Frosting
400g full-fat cream cheese
100g icing sugar
finely grated zest and juice
    of half an orange
100g pecan halves to decorate

You will also need a 25 x 20cm baking tin, greased and lined with baking parchment

Preheat the oven to 180°C/350°F/Gas Mark 4.

Mix together the sugar and oil using either an electric hand whisk or in the bowl of a free-standing mixer. Add the eggs and mix until smooth.

Using a large metal spoon, fold in the flour, mixed spice and a pinch of salt.

Add the grated carrot, chopped pecans and orange zest and mix until thoroughly combined. Spoon into the prepared tin and bake on the middle shelf of the preheated oven for 30–40 minutes until golden and a wooden skewer inserted into the middle of the cake comes out clean.

Prepare the orange syrup. In a small saucepan, heat the orange juice and caster sugar until the sugar has dissolved and the liquid has reduced by one-third.

Brush the warm cake with the warm orange syrup and leave until completely cold.

To make the frosting, beat the cream cheese, icing sugar, orange zest and orange juice until smooth.

Once the cake has cooled, spread over the frosting with a palette knife and scatter with pecan halves to serve.

APRICOT LOAF

This started off as a soaked sultana loaf that my Auntie Helen has made for as long as I can remember. She is the most lovely lady, the type you'd want to spend time with; she radiates kindness from every pore, so I thought I'd try a variation on the theme as a tribute to her.

300g dried apricots
300g caster sugar
200g unsalted butter, very soft
1 tsp almond essence
3 large eggs, beaten
300g self-raising flour
a pinch of salt
4 tbsp demerara sugar

You will also need a 900g (2lb) loaf tin, the inside buttered and the base and ends lined with a strip of buttered baking parchment

Preheat the oven to 170°C/325°F/Gas Mark 3.

Chop the apricots into 1cm pieces and tip into a bowl. Cover with hot water and leave to soak for 10 minutes.

Strain the apricots and pat dry on kitchen paper. Return to the bowl and add the sugar, butter and almond essence and stir until the butter has melted.

Mix in the eggs and then fold in the flour and a pinch of salt.

Spoon into the prepared tin and spread level. Sprinkle with the demerara sugar and bake on the middle shelf of the preheated oven for 60–70 minutes until well risen and golden brown, and a wooden skewer inserted into the middle of the cake comes out clean. Cover with foil if the cake starts to brown too quickly.

Cool on a wire rack before cutting into slices to serve.

BANANA LOAF

This is a great loaf: I've made it more times than I care to remember, and it's one of those staple cakes that never fails me. It has been on my blog now for a long time and lots of people requested that I put it in the book, so here it is. Sometimes I make it in a 1lb loaf tin and use the rest in those mini loaf tins with muffin cases jiggled into them, perfect for a packed lunch box.

100g demerara sugar
150g soft light brown sugar
2 large eggs
2 ripe bananas, mashed
280g plain flour
2 tsp baking powder
140g unsalted butter, melted
50g pecans, chopped
2 tsp ground cinnamon

You will also need a 900g (2lb) loaf tin, the inside buttered and the base and ends lined with a strip of buttered baking parchment

Preheat the oven to 170°C/325°F/Gas Mark 3.

Whisk the demerara and soft light brown sugar with the eggs until thoroughly combined. Mix in the mashed banana.

Sift the flour and baking powder into the bowl and fold in using a large metal spoon.

Add the melted butter and mix until thoroughly combined.

Spoon the batter into the prepared tin and scatter with the chopped pecans and ground cinnamon. Bake on the middle shelf of the preheated oven for about 1 hour or until a wooden skewer inserted into the middle of the cake comes out clean. Cover the cake with foil if it appears to be browning too quickly.

Remove the cake from the tin and leave to cool on a wire rack.

CHOCOLATE, CARDAMOM AND STRAWBERRY SWISS ROLL

I love the flavour of a little cardamom with strawberries and chocolate: it is truly a marriage made in heaven.

4 large eggs

100g caster sugar, plus
   3 tbsp for sprinkling

40g cocoa powder

40g self-raising flour

25g cornflour

300g strawberries,
   hulled and sliced

3 tbsp cardamom sugar
   (see pages 248–9)

300ml double cream

150ml Greek yogurt

1 tsp orange zest,
   finely grated

50g white chocolate,
   finely grated

You will also need a 30 x 23cm Swiss roll tin lined with buttered baking parchment

Preheat the oven to 180°C/350°F/Gas Mark 4.

Using a free-standing mixer, whisk together the eggs and 100g of caster sugar until pale, light and fluffy. The mixture should double in volume.

Sieve the cocoa, flour and cornflour into another bowl and fold into the egg mixture, one third at a time, using a large metal spoon.

Carefully spoon the mixture into the prepared tin and bake on the middle shelf of the oven for about 10–12 minutes until puffy and well risen.

Lay a large sheet of baking parchment on the work surface and sprinkle with 3 tablespoons of caster sugar.

Turn out of the tin onto the parchment and peel off the baking paper. Roll the cake up, starting from one of the short ends, and with the sugared parchment inside the sponge. Cover with a slightly damp tea towel and leave to cool.

Sprinkle the strawberries with half of the cardamom sugar and leave to one side for 5 minutes.

Whip together the cream, Greek yogurt, orange zest and remaining cardamom sugar until it forms soft peaks.

Carefully unroll the sponge. Sprinkle with the white chocolate and lay the strawberries over them. Spread the cream mixture over the strawberries and re-roll the sponge as tightly as possible.

Cut into slices to serve.

Family baking

AFTERNOON TEA

*I adore afternoon tea, it's so quintessentially British.
It makes me smile. I've always rather fancied it at The Ritz
but have never quite made it, though I hope that one day
soon I will get to try those light-as-a-feather sandwiches
and delicate little pastries, all served on silver salvers.
(Well, the truth is that I have no idea if that's how they
actually present them, but a girl can dream, can't she?)*

♥

MINI PISTACHIO MERINGUES

These were one of my final bakes for The Great British Bake Off. *I was fast asleep when I came up with the idea: I'd been to Sainsbury's the evening before and found some freeze-dried raspberry white chocolate and bought it without knowing how I was going to use it. The next morning I jumped out of bed and couldn't wait to try it out, and it really didn't disappoint. If you can't find this particular chocolate, you can use freeze-dried raspberries and add them to the melted white chocolate. You can buy freeze-dried raspberries very easily online.*

3 egg whites
1 tbsp lemon juice
150g caster sugar
30g pistachios, shelled,
unsalted and finely chopped
100g white chocolate with
freeze-dried raspberry pieces
150ml double cream, whipped
30 fresh raspberries
30 mint leaves (tiny ones)

You will also need a baking tray lined with baking parchment and a piping bag fitted with a small plain nozzle

Preheat the oven to 110°C/225°F/Gas Mark ¼.

In a spotlessly clean, dry bowl, whisk the egg whites to soft peaks and add the lemon juice.

Gradually fold in the sugar, then add the nuts by gently folding in using a large metal spoon.

Spoon into the piping bag, and pipe little nests onto the prepared baking tray, about 3cm wide and 3cm high.

Bake for about 1 hour, until dry and crisp. Turn the oven off and leave the meringues to cool inside.

Melt the raspberry chocolate in a heatproof bowl. Stir until smooth and brush the insides of the meringue nests, then leave to set. Whip the cream to soft peaks, spoon into a piping bag and pipe little swirls onto the nests.

Top each meringue nest with a raspberry followed by a mint leaf.

CHOCOLATE CHEESECAKE MINI CUPCAKES

These are so lovely and light that you almost certainly won't be able to restrict yourself to just the one. They're perfect for sharing with a group of your best friends, and I'd like to dedicate this recipe to my Monday girls.

120g plain flour
140g caster sugar
1 tsp baking powder
½ tsp bicarbonate of soda
40g butter
110ml full-fat milk
1 egg, beaten
1 tsp vanilla extract
50g dark chocolate,
   melted and cooled

Cream-cheese topping
3 Bourbon biscuits
100g full-fat cream cheese
1 tsp vanilla extract
125g unsalted butter, softened
500g icing sugar
30 chocolate buttons

You will also need 30 mini cupcake cases, a baking tray and a piping bag fitted with a small plain nozzle

Preheat oven to 170°C/325°F/ Gas Mark 3.

In the bowl of a free-standing machine add flour, sugar, baking powder and bicarbonate of soda and give a quick mix.

Add the butter and combine until you have a sandy consistency. Add half the milk and blend.

Mix together the rest of the milk, egg and vanilla extract and pour slowly into the batter. Mix in the melted chocolate until well combined and stir until smooth.

Spoon into 30 mini cupcake cases. Place on a baking tray and bake in the preheated oven for about 15 minutes.

Cool on wire racks until cold.

Blend the Bourbon biscuits in a food processor or put into a plastic sandwich bag and bash with a rolling pin until you have fine crumbs.

Mix together the cream cheese, vanilla extract, butter and icing sugar in a free-standing machine until light and fluffy, then spoon into a piping bag fitted with a star nozzle.

Pipe cream-cheese frosting into a swirl onto the cupcakes and top with a sprinkle of the biscuit crumbs.

Top each cake with a chocolate button; I like a mix of white and milk.

Afternoon tea

MINI BANOFFEE PIES

These are lovely chewy, chocolatey, banana toffee delights, really light and perfect for afternoon tea. The mousse works so well, it's almost a lighter play on the original, a banana lover's delight.

8 digestive biscuits
80g unsalted butter

Toffee
20g butter
120g brown sugar
100ml double cream

Banana mousse
2 ripe bananas
4 tbsp icing sugar
250ml double cream
50g dark chocolate
   for shavings

You will also need a 12-hole muffin tin lined with paper cases and a piping bag fitted with a medium nozzle

Preheat the oven to 180°C/350°F/Gas Mark 4.

Crush the digestive biscuits either in a food processor or put into a sandwich bag and bash with a rolling pin.

Melt 80g of the butter and mix together with the biscuits until thoroughly combined. Spoon into a muffin tin lined with 12 cases.

Bake on the middle shelf of the preheated oven for 5 minutes.

Cool and put the tin in the fridge to chill.

To make the toffee, melt the butter and sugar in a pan, and add in the cream. Bring to the boil and simmer for a few minutes until the sugar has dissolved. Pour into a container and chill.

Mash the bananas and add the icing sugar.

Whip the cream to soft peaks, add the banana purée and fold in until smooth.

Once the biscuit bases have set, place a tablespoon of toffee onto each one. — *chill 'til set before next step*

Spoon the banana mousse into a piping bag and pipe swirls onto the tops. Finish with dark chocolate shavings or a dusting of cocoa.

Chill for at least 1 hour before serving.

MINI MISSISSIPPI MUD PIES

You can't really go wrong with this combination of short chocolate pastry shells with soft, brownie-type centres, softly whipped white cream and grated dark chocolate: a sure-fire hit with children and adults alike.

Pastry
130g plain flour
20g cocoa
2 tbsp icing sugar
a pinch of salt
75g unsalted butter,
    chilled and diced
1 large egg yolk, beaten
1–3 tbsp cold water

Filling
100g dark chocolate,
    chopped into small pieces
30g unsalted butter
20ml golden syrup
60ml double cream
150g caster sugar
3 large eggs, beaten

To finish
200ml double cream, whipped
50g chocolate, grated

You will also need a 12-hole patty/bun tin and 7.5cm round cutters

Preheat the oven to 180°C/350°F/ Gas Mark 4.

Blitz flour, cocoa, icing sugar, salt and butter in a food processor until the mixture resembles fine sand.

Bring together to form a dough with egg yolk and water as needed. Turn out and knead for 30 seconds, then wrap the dough in cling film and chill for half an hour.

Lightly dust the work surface with flour and roll out the dough to a thickness of no more than 2mm. Use a cutter to stamp out 12 rounds and divide between the 12 patty tins. Line each pastry case with a square of tinfoil and blind bake on the middle shelf of the oven for 10 minutes until firm.

Remove the pastry and turn the oven down to 190°C/375°F/ Gas Mark 5.

In a bowl over some boiling water, melt the chocolate, butter, golden syrup and cream together, and stir until smooth and shiny. Remove from the heat.

Whisk the sugar and eggs together and pour into the chocolate mixture, stirring until well combined. Pour the chocolate mixture into the pastry cases and bake on the middle shelf for 15 minutes, or until the filling has set.

Leave in the tins until cool and chill for at least a couple of hours.

Top with whipped double cream and scatter with some chocolate shavings.

CHOCOLATE, CHERRY AND ORANGE FRIANDS

I first tried a friand about twenty years ago in London's West End. While waiting for some friends, I popped into a little cafe and wanted something small to go with my coffee, so the barista recommended that I try one of these gorgeous almond treats. I was hooked at once and tried for ages to recreate that loveliness, and I now think I have finally matched the one I remember from all those years ago. The specially shaped tins referred to here are readily available online, but a muffin tin will work just as well as long as it's well greased and you fill the holes no more than a little over half full.

85g plain flour

150g icing sugar, plus
    extra for dusting

1 tsp baking powder

30g cocoa

100g ground almonds

5 egg whites, lightly whisked

50g dark chocolate,
    melted and cooled

200g unsalted butter, melted

zest of 1 orange

100g dried cherries

**You will also need a
12-hole friand or muffin
tin, buttered and lightly
dusted with plain flour**

Preheat the oven to 170°C/325°F/Gas Mark 3.

Sift the flour, icing sugar, baking powder, cocoa and ground almonds into a mixing bowl and stir to combine.

Stir in the egg whites.

Fold in the chocolate and melted butter using a metal spoon or spatula.

Stir in the orange zest and cherries until thoroughly combined.

Spoon into prepared friand tins.

Bake for 20 minutes or until the mixture springs back when touched.

Cool in the tins for 3–4 minutes and then turn out onto a wire cooling rack until cold. Lightly dust with icing sugar to serve.

MINI MINT CHOC CHIP SHOTS

These little creamy shots came about in memory of a childhood moment when my brother Mark and I had been at the home of Kathy and Mick, our honorary aunt and uncle – an unforgettable day when they gave us our first taste of chocolate mint-chip ice cream and we played in the garden with a sprinkler that created a lovely little rainbow.

200ml double cream
200g full-fat cream cheese
a small amount of green
    food colouring or gel
4 tbsp icing sugar
1 tbsp peppermint essence
30g dark mint chocolate,
    grated coarsely
3 Bourbon biscuits broken
    into crumbs
6 mint leaves

You will also need 6 small
shot glasses and a piping
bag fitted with a 1cm nozzle

Whip the cream to soft peaks, then fold in the cream cheese, food colouring, sugar and peppermint essence. Taste to test the flavour.

Fold in the chocolate shavings.

In small shot glasses, add a teaspoon of biscuit crumbs.

Spoon cream mixture into a piping bag and pipe into the glasses. Top with some biscuit crumbs.

Chill for up to half an hour, then serve topped with a little mint leaf.

HONEY AND ALMOND TARTS

I think it's really great when you create different textures and tastes in a bake, and these little tarts do just that, with soft, short, crumbly pastry, then sticky honey and crunchy almonds, all topped off with tangy lemon icing. What's more, it's really simple.

Pastry
200g plain flour, plus
   extra for rolling out
a pinch of salt
2 tbsp icing sugar
100g unsalted butter,
   chilled and diced
1 large egg yolk, beaten
1–3 tbsp cold water

Filling
60g unsalted butter
60g granulated sugar
2 tbsp clear honey
1 tbsp double cream
90g flaked almonds
200g icing sugar
zest and juice of 1 lemon

You will also need a 12-hole patty/bun tin and 7.5cm round cutters

Make the pastry first. Blitz the flour, salt, icing sugar and butter together in a food processor.

Add the egg yolk and just enough water to bring the dough together.

Turn out the dough onto the work surface, wrap in cling film and chill for half an hour.

In a saucepan gently heat the butter, sugar and honey together, and bring to the boil.

Remove from the heat and stir in the cream and almonds, then put aside to cool.

Roll out the pastry onto a surface lightly dusted with flour, to a thickness of no more than 2mm. Cut out 12 rounds using the cutter and press into the patty tins. Chill in the fridge for 15 minutes.

Preheat oven to 180°C/350°F/Gas Mark 4.

Spoon in the almond mix and bake on the middle shelf of the preheated oven for 20 minutes.

Cool until firmed up in the patty tins, then transfer to cool completely on wire racks.

Mix together icing sugar, half of the lemon zest and enough lemon juice to make a firm paste.

Spoon onto the tartlets to cover the tops completely and leave to set, topping with a little lemon zest to serve.

CHEESE AND ONION CHUTNEY SCONES

Scones remind me of my lovely friend Maria, whom I first met at antenatal class. There were nine of us in the group, and we used to gather every Tuesday with our older children, sometimes as many as 18 of them. When it was 'Auntie' Maria's turn to do the catering, she always baked scones. I adore onion and marmalade: the savoury and sweet work really well together, like yin and yang. These scones should be served with lashings of cold unsalted butter.

225g self-raising flour
1 tsp cream of tartar
½ tsp bicarbonate of soda
a pinch of salt
50g unsalted butter,
    diced and chilled
65g onion chutney
85g cheddar cheese, grated
150ml full-fat milk
1 egg yolk, beaten
plain flour for dusting

You will also need a baking tray lined with baking parchment and a 6–7cm plain round cutter

Preheat oven to 220°C/425°F/Gas Mark 7.

Sift the flour, cream of tartar, bicarbonate of soda and salt into a large mixing bowl.

Rub in the butter until the mixture looks like fine sand.

Add the onion chutney and cheese, then slowly add the milk, using a knife to mix the ingredients together.

Turn out the dough onto a floured surface and give it a little knead for about 20 seconds: don't overwork, as this makes a heavy scone.

Roll out to a thickness of about 2–3cm and, using a 6–7cm cutter cut into rounds, and put onto the prepared baking tray.

Brush with the beaten egg.

Bake for 12–14 minutes until well risen and golden.

Cool on a wire rack and serve warm.

CRANBERRY AND ORANGE SCONES

I've been using this basic scone recipe for as long as I can remember: it's like an old friend, one you can always rely on, the sort who never lets you down, and we all need one of those from time to time. I fancied giving this familiar face a makeover and the results were delicious: the zing of the orange zest, the soft scone and the crunch of the sugary top really make it a winning combination.

225g self-raising flour
1 tsp cream of tartar
½ tsp bicarbonate of soda
1 tbsp caster sugar
a pinch of salt
50g unsalted butter,
   chilled and diced
zest and juice of 1 orange
50g dried cranberries
full-fat milk
1 egg yolk, beaten
4 tbsp demerara sugar

You will also need a baking tray lined with baking parchment and a 6cm round cutter

Preheat oven to 210°C/410°F/ Gas Mark 6.

Sift the flour, cream of tartar, bicarbonate of soda, sugar and salt into a bowl.

Rub in the butter with your fingers until the mixture resembles fine breadcrumbs. Add the orange zest and cranberries.

In a jug, pour in the freshly squeezed orange juice then add enough milk to make 150ml of liquid.

Gradually add to the dry mixture and work together with a knife. Finish by bringing together with your hands.

Turn out onto a floured surface and give it a little knead for 20 seconds (too much working will make tough scones), then roll out your dough to a thickness of 2–3cm.

Using a 6cm cutter, cut into rounds and put them onto the prepared baking tray. Brush with the beaten egg and sprinkle with demerara sugar.

Bake on the middle shelf of the preheated oven for 12–14 minutes.

Cool on a wire rack until ready to eat.

CHEESE STRAWS

Cheese straws remind me of being a little girl and of Christmas parties at my Nanny Jess's house, with Slade and Chas & Dave blaring on the record player. My brother and I were the youngest and we had to wait until all the older cousins got back from my auntie and uncle's pub: it was then that the knees-up began. My nan had eight children, each of whom had at least two children of their own, so you can imagine this was a really big family occasion. There were lots of bakes, hanging decorations, cards on strings, my older cousins in all in the latest fashions ... it was the highlight of my childhood Christmases.

60g unsalted butter, chilled
60g cheddar cheese, grated
150g plain flour
a pinch of salt
½ tsp mustard powder
1 tbsp light olive or
    sunflower oil
3 tbsp cold fizzy water
1 large egg, beaten
4 tbsp chutney, heated and
    passed through a sieve
2 tbsp sesame seeds

**You will also need a baking
tray lined with parchment**

Preheat oven to 200°C/400°F/Gas Mark 6.

In a food processor, combine the butter, cheese, flour, salt and mustard powder.

Pour in the oil and fizzy water and process until the dough starts to come together.

Turn out onto a lightly floured surface, and bring together into a smooth ball.

Roll out the pastry into an oblong with a thickness of about 4mm and cut into 10cm x 2cm strips. Twist each strip gently a couple of times and lay on a baking tray.

Brush the straws with the beaten egg, taking care not to untwist them.

Bake on the middle shelf of the preheated oven for 12–18 minutes until golden.

Leave to cool on baking trays until cooled and firm.

Brush one end of each twist with the warm, sieved chutney.

Dip into sesame seeds.

Leave to set on a wire rack.

HAZELNUT AND ORANGE MACAROONS

Ever since I discovered macaroons I've struggled to conquer my fascination with them. They are tricky to make but please keep trying because once you get the hang of it, you never lose the knack. I'd suggest undermixing for your first batch, then adding an extra fold at each subsequent attempt: rest assured that if you work at it you'll get there in the end.

15g ground hazelnuts
70g ground almonds
115g icing sugar
2 large egg whites
50g caster sugar
a little orange food
    colouring gel

Filling
100g icing sugar
2 tbsp Nutella
zest of 1 orange
25g icing sugar

You will also need a large
piping bag fitted with a plain
1cm nozzle and 2 baking trays
lined with baking parchment

Preheat the oven to 160°C/320°F/Gas Mark 3.

Blend the ground hazelnuts, ground almonds and icing sugar for about 30 seconds in a food processor. Sieve into a bowl.

In a clean, dry mixing bowl, whisk the egg whites into soft peaks, then slowly add the caster sugar, whisking well between each addition. Add the food colouring and continue to whisk until firm and glossy.

Fold in the almond mixture one third at a time with a metal spoon. Continue to fold the mixture until you have a glossy batter that falls in ribbons.

Spoon into a piping bag and pipe 28 small rounds onto the prepared baking trays.

Tap the baking trays firmly on the work surface to knock out any air bubbles and leave to rest, uncovered, to form a skin for 1 hour.

Bake the macaroons one tray at a time on the middle shelf of the oven for 12–15 minutes, or until firm. Remove from the oven and cool on the tray until totally cold.

Mix filling ingredients together in a free-standing machine until soft and fluffy, and use to sandwich the macaroon pairs together.

PINEAPPLE AND COCONUT MACAROONS

This year I was in London with my lovely friends Di, Heather and Sara for Di's 50th birthday celebrations. We had lunch and then decided to have dessert in Ladurée. We picked out ten macaroons and cut them into quarters so we could each try all of them.

15g desiccated coconut
70g ground almonds
115g icing sugar
2 large egg whites
50g caster sugar
a little yellow food
    colouring gel, optional

Filling
100g icing sugar
2 tbsp creamed coconut
2 tbsp puréed pineapple,
    tinned or fresh
25g icing sugar

You will also need a large
piping bag fitted with a plain
1cm nozzle and 2 baking trays
lined with baking parchment

Preheat oven to 160°C/320°F/Gas Mark 3.

Blend the coconut, ground almonds and icing sugar for about 30 seconds in a food processor. Sieve into a bowl.

In a clean, dry mixing bowl, whisk the egg whites into soft peaks, then slowly add the caster sugar, beating well between each addition. Add the food colouring if you're using it and continue to whisk until firm and glossy.

Fold in almond mixture one third at a time with a metal spoon. Continue to fold in a cutting or figure-of-eight movement with the metal spoon until you have a glossy batter.

Spoon into a piping bag and pipe 28 small rounds onto the prepared baking trays.

Tap the baking trays firmly on the work surface to knock out any air bubbles and leave to rest, uncovered, to form a skin for 1 hour.

Bake the macaroons, one tray at a time, on the middle shelf of the oven for 12–15 minutes, or until firm.

Cool on the tray for at least 10 minutes.

Combine filling ingredients together in a freestanding machine until soft and fluffy, then sandwich macaroon pairs together.

CROSTINI

Crostini are fab: they are such versatile little things. All you need is a day-old baguette and you're halfway there. These little crostini hit all the right notes.

1 day-old baguette sliced into 2cm vertical slices
3–4 tbsp olive oil
1 clove of garlic
rock salt

Preheat oven to 200°C/400°F/Gas Mark 6.

Brush the baguette slices with olive oil.

Cut the garlic clove in half and rub along each slice.

Sprinkle with rock salt.

Place on baking trays.

Bake for 10–12 minutes, turning over halfway through, until golden brown.

Cool on wire racks until totally cold.

Goats' cheese and onion marmalade crostini

For me, goats cheese and onion marmalade are a match made in heaven.

MAKES 6
6 crostini bases
6 tsp onion marmalade
150g goats' cheese
olive oil
a few thyme leaves

Preheat the grill.

Arrange the crostini bases onto a baking tray and spread a teaspoon of onion marmalade onto each slice.

Crumble equal amounts of goats' cheese over each crostini.

Drizzle over half a teaspoon of olive oil and top with some fresh thyme.

Grill until the cheese starts to bubble (or, if you prefer, put onto a baking tray in a preheated oven to 220°C/425°F/Gas Mark 7 for about 6–8 minutes.

Serve hot or warm.

Mozzarella and roasted pepper crostini
A taste of the Med in a flash

MAKES 6
a small jar of roasted peppers
6 crostini bases
6 basil leaves, plus 6 to finish
150g mozzarella, drained
olive oil

Preheat the grill.

Drain the peppers and chop into medium-sized pieces; divide between the crostini bases and arrange on a baking tray.

Rip the basil leaves into small pieces and scatter on top of the peppers.

Top with chunks of mozzarella.

Drizzle with oil and flash under a hot grill until the cheese just starts to melt.

Top with a basil leaf to serve.

Mushroom crostini
Lovely creamy mushrooms with crisp toasted bases

MAKES 6
30g butter
2 tbsp olive oil
200g button mushrooms, sliced
1 shallot, diced finely
1 clove of garlic, crushed
4 tbsp double cream
6 crostini bases
2 tbsp Parmesan shavings
flat leaf parsley, chopped

Melt the butter in a saucepan along with the olive oil.

Add the sliced mushrooms, chopped shallot and garlic, and cook for about 10 minutes over a medium heat or until mushrooms are tender.

Add the double cream; bring to the boil and reduce down until quite thick and creamy. Season with salt and freshly ground pepper.

Spoon the mushroom mixture onto the crostini bases and top with Parmesan shavings and chopped parsley to serve.

Chapter
five

CELEBRATION BAKES

I so love making a special cake: it gives an air of excitement to any big occasion. I particularly look forward to Christmas and the fun of getting all my fruits into their little boozy bath; I've used the same recipe for the last twenty-four years. Wedding cakes are also great, and when some friends asked me to make theirs I felt honoured and proud that they were entrusting me with one of the keys to the success of their big day. And then of course there are birthday cakes – I always made them for my boys when they were little and you can be sure that all the children will love anything from a simple chocolate cake covered in their favourite sweeties to the most elaborate Thunderbirds rocket.

CHRISTMAS PUDDING

This recipe started out as Delia's but it has been jiggled about with for so many years that I think I can now call it my own. That's the wonderful thing about baking — with confidence, you can make any recipe your own.

1 Bramley cooking apple
50g blanched almonds
80g suet
40g unsalted butter, melted
110g fresh breadcrumbs
200g soft dark brown sugar
500g dried fruits (sultanas,
   currants, raisins, dried
   cherries, apricots . . .
   whatever takes your fancy
   really, but use a base of
   sultanas, currants and
   raisins, at least 400g)
30g mixed peel paste
   (see pages 248–9)
2 tsp mixed spice
finely grated zest and juice
   of 1 small orange
finely grated zest of one lemon
2 large eggs, beaten
120ml stout
3 tbsp brandy

You will also need a 1.2 litre
(2 pint) pudding basin, buttered

Start this recipe the day before you plan to steam your pudding. Peel, core and finely chop the apple and tip into a large mixing bowl. Chop the almonds and add to the bowl with the suet, butter, breadcrumbs, sugar, dried fruit and mixed peel paste. Add the mixed spice and grated orange and lemon zest and mix well.

Mix the eggs, orange juice, stout and brandy together in a small jug and pour into the bowl stirring well; I always get the boys to give the mixture a good stir and a wish at this point. Cover with cling film and leave overnight for the flavours to develop.

The next day spoon into the pudding basin and cover with a double layer of baking parchment and a sheet of foil, fold a pleat in the middle and fold the paper and foil over the sides of the bowl. Tie securely with kitchen string.

Put the bowl either into a steamer pan or in a large saucepan with an upturned saucer in the bottom. Pour boiling water into the pan to come halfway up the sides of the bowl, and steam for 8 hours, checking regularly that the water doesn't run dry.

Remove the pudding from the pan and leave it to go cold. Cover with fresh paper and foil and store in a cool, dark place until you are ready to reheat and serve.

Re-steam the pudding for 3 hours to serve with brandy butter.

Any leftover pudding can be stored in the fridge, wrapped in foil and reheated in the oven.

CHRISTMAS CAKE

Christmas is the one time of year when you know you're all going to get together, play silly games, eat the hugest dinner in the world and watch repeats of films and sitcoms on TV. And the weeks of shopping that precede it! I remember queuing outside Toys R Us at 5 a.m. to get the latest thing ... But it was all worth it when they tore off the wrappings on Christmas morning and you could just tell from their faces that you'd got it right.

500g mixed dried fruit
100g glacé cherries, halved
8 tbsp brandy, plus extra
    for feeding the cake
175g unsalted butter, softened
100g soft light brown sugar
75g soft dark brown sugar
4 large eggs, beaten
250g self-raising flour
3 tsp mixed spice
3 tbsp black treacle
70g mixed peel paste
    (see page 249)

You will also need a
20cm-deep cake tin,
greased and lined with
baking parchment and
the outside of the tin
wrapped in a piece
of brown paper tied
with string

Soak the dried fruit and glacé cherries in 8 tablespoons of brandy overnight.

Preheat the oven to 170°C/325°F/Gas Mark 3.

In the bowl of a free-standing mixer, cream the butter and both of the sugars until light and fluffy. Gradually add the beaten eggs, mixing well between each addition.

Using a large metal spoon, fold the flour and spices into the mixture. Add the dried fruits, black treacle and mixed peel paste and mix until thoroughly combined.

Spoon into the tin and spread level. Bake in the bottom half of the oven for 90 minutes and then turn the heat down to 150°C/300°F/Gas Mark 2 and continue baking for a further hour. If the cake is browning too quickly, cover the top with foil. The cake is cooked when a wooden skewer inserted into the middle of the cake comes out clean.

Cool in the tin for 20 minutes, then turn out and transfer to a wire rack to cool completely.

Prick the bottom of the cake with a cocktail stick and feed with a couple of tablespoons of brandy.

Wrap in parchment paper and a layer of tin foil. Feed over the next few weeks before covering with marzipan and icing.

Celebration bakes

MINCEMEAT

Years ago I started making my own mincemeat and I've never used the shop bought stuff again. I promise you will feel the same after tasting it!

1 Bramley cooking apple,
   diced, peeled and cored
650g raisins, sultanas,
   currants, apricots, dried
   cherries, dried cranberries
100g mixed chopped nuts
   (hazelnuts, almonds
   and pecans are all fab)
25g mixed peel paste
   (see pages 248–9)
5 tsp mixed spice
125g soft light brown sugar
125g suet or unsalted
   butter, melted
zest and juice of 1 orange
zest of 1 lemon
3 tbsp brandy

Preheat the oven to 150°C/300°F/Gas Mark 2.

Tip the apple into a large heatproof bowl or roasting tin. Add the remaining ingredients apart from the brandy, cover with foil and place in the preheated oven for about 1 hour or until combined and the fruit is juicy.

Leave to cool slightly, add the brandy and stir to combine. Once the mincemeat is cold, store in an airtight box in the fridge for up to 3 months.

MINCE PIES

Oh, truly for me the queen of Christmas treats!

250g plain flour, plus
    extra for rolling out
125g unsalted butter,
    chilled and cubed
a pinch of salt
1 large egg yolk, beaten
⅔ tbsp chilled water
12 dessertspoonfuls
    of mincemeat
1 egg, beaten with 1 tbsp water
caster sugar for sprinkling

**You will also need a 12-hole
bun tin and fluted cutters:
7.5cm and 6cm**

Preheat oven to 190°C/375°F/Gas Mark 5.

Put the flour, butter and salt into the bowl of
a food processor fitted with the metal blade.
Whizz using the pulse button until you have
a breadcrumb consistency.

Add the egg yolk, whizz briefly and then add
the chilled water, one tablespoon at a time,
until the dough comes together.

Turn onto a lightly floured work surface and
work very briefly with your hands until smooth.
Wrap in cling film and chill for at least 30 minutes
before using.

Turn the pastry out onto a lightly floured work
surface and roll out to a thickness of no more than
2mm. Using the cutters stamp out 12 x 7.5cm discs
and 12 x 6cm discs. Line the bun tin with the larger
pastry discs, pressing the pastry well into the
corners and brush the edges with egg wash. Spoon
the mincemeat into each case and top with the
smaller pastry discs pressing the edges to seal.

Brush with egg wash, sprinkle with caster sugar
and bake for 25 minutes on the middle shelf of
the preheated oven.

Leave the pies in the tins to firm up for 5 minutes
and then transfer onto wire racks to cool.

VALENTINE'S CHOCOLATE SHORTBREAD HEARTS

These are lovely crisp, fruity desserts, so perfect for a romantic evening. You can make the biscuits a day or two before and the sauce can be made and chilled in the morning, then it's just an assembly job of about two minutes.

Shortbread
50g plain flour, plus
extra for rolling out
50g unsalted butter,
chilled and diced
25g cocoa powder
25g caster sugar

Filling
100g raspberries
50g icing sugar, plus
extra for dusting
100ml double cream
100g strawberries
white chocolate shavings
or cocoa to serve

You will also need a 7.5cm heart-shaped cookie cutter and a piping bag fitted with a medium star nozzle

Preheat the oven to 170°C/325°F/Gas Mark 3.

Tip all of the shortbread ingredients into a food processor and whizz until you have a soft dough. Flatten into a disc, wrap in cling film and chill for at least 30 minutes.

Dust the work surface with flour and roll out the shortbread dough to a thickness of 2–3mm and stamp out 6 hearts using the cookie cutter. Arrange on a lined tray and bake on the middle shelf of the oven for 12–13 minutes until firm. Keep a very close eye on them as even a slight burn will make the shortbread taste bitter.

Leave to cool and firm slightly before transferring onto a wire rack to cool completely.

Mash the raspberries with a fork and then push through a sieve to remove the pips. Add icing sugar to taste. Whip the cream until it will hold a peak and spoon into the piping bag fitted with a star nozzle. Hull and slice the strawberries.

To assemble the shortbreads, spread a couple of spoonfuls of the raspberry purée onto each plate and place one shortbread heart on top. Pipe cream on top of the shortbread and arrange sliced strawberries on top of this. Top with a second shortbread and repeat this layering.

Sprinkle with a little icing sugar, white chocolate shavings or cocoa, and serve with the rest of the raspberry purée on the side.

Celebration bakes

BABY SHOWER GIANT CUPCAKE

Blue for a boy, pink for a girl or half-and-half if you don't know yet!

375g self-raising flour
375g caster sugar
375g margarine
6 large eggs, beaten
1 x 500g packet of candy
   melts in pink, blue or the
   speckled pink and blue
1 large pack of Smarties

Buttercream
600g icing sugar
125g unsalted butter, softened
1 tsp vanilla extract
⅔ tbsp full-fat milk
pink or blue gel colours
200g fondant, pink or blue

**You will also need a giant
cupcake tin, well greased with
Dr Oetker Cake Release Spray
and a large piping bag fitted
with a large star nozzle**

Flavoured sugars
I always have about 6 jars
of flavoured sugars in my
cupboard, to add a little extra
something to your bakes.
See pages 248–9 for ideas.

Preheat the oven to 170°C/325°F/Gas Mark 3.

Tip the flour, sugar, margarine and eggs into the bowl
of a free-standing mixer and beat until light and fluffy.
Spoon the mixture into the prepared tin and bake just
below the middle of the for about 1 hour, or until a skewer
inserted into the middle of the cake comes out clean.
Turn the cake out onto a wire rack to cool.

Wash, dry and grease the cake tin again; this time you
will only need the bottom half.

Heat a packet of candy melts according to the pack
instructions and stir until smooth. Brush the bottom
half of the cupcake tin with the melted candy in a smooth
and even layer, and leave in the fridge to chill and set.

To remove the candy cupcake shell from the tin, fill the
sink with very hot water and dip the bottom of the cake
tin into it. Gently release the shell and place on a serving
plate. Place the bottom half of the sponge into the shell,
trimming to fit. Carefully place the cupcake sponge on top.

To make the buttercream, combine the icing sugar,
butter, vanilla extract and milk in the bowl of the
free-standing mixer and beat until light and fluffy.
Divide the buttercream between two mixing bowls
and tint one bowl either pink or blue using the gel
colours. Spoon alternate colours of buttercream into
a large piping bag fitted with a large star nozzle.

Pipe little stars around the join of the two cakes and
then starting from the bottom pipe large rosettes of
buttercream all over the top cake to completely cover.
Fill in any gaps with small stars of buttercream.

To finish tie a pretty ribbon around the cupcake.

MINI COFFEE AND WALNUT MACAROONS

I love these little guys: perfect to serve with coffee after a special dinner. They're one of those things you can't resist even when you're full.

50g pecans
50g ground almonds
115g icing sugar
2 large egg whites
50g caster sugar
1 tsp Camp coffee

Buttercream filling
200g icing sugar
50g unsalted butter, softened
1 tbsp Camp coffee
⅔ tbsp full-fat milk
20g dark chocolate, grated

You will also need a large piping bag fitted with a 1cm plain nozzle and 2 large baking trays lined with baking parchment

Preheat the oven to 170°C/325°F/Gas Mark 3.

Finely chop the pecans and whizz in a food processor with the ground almonds and icing sugar, for 1 minute until thoroughly combined.

In a large mixing bowl, whisk the egg whites until they will hold a soft peak. Gradually add the caster sugar, mixing well between each addition. Using a large metal spoon, fold the almond mixture into the egg whites, one third at a time, and then add the coffee.

Continue to fold until the batter is smooth and shiny. Spoon the mixture into the prepared piping bag and pipe 25 small, even-sized rounds onto each prepared baking tray – about 2cm in diameter each. Tap the bottom of the baking trays sharply and firmly on the work surface to remove any air bubbles from the mixture and leave at room temperature for about 30 minutes, or until a skin has formed on the top.

Bake on the middle shelf of the oven for about 7–9 minutes until the tops are firm and crisp. Remove from the oven and leave on the trays until totally cold.

To make the buttercream filling, cream together all of the ingredients until light and fluffy. Spoon into a piping bag fitted with the 1cm nozzle and pipe small rounds onto the flat side of half of the macaroon shells. Sprinkle the buttercream with grated dark chocolate and top with matching macaroon shells.

CHOCOLATE FAVOURS

I was messing around in the kitchen when the idea of these just popped into my head. They are simple and really versatile. I'm going to give you the quantity of ingredients for ten so it is easy to multiply.

150g dark chocolate
40g toasted hazelnuts,
    chopped
15g demerara sugar
zest of 1 orange

You will need a disposable piping bag, a large baking tray covered with baking parchment and 10 paper lolly sticks

Children's lollies
For children's lollies you can use the same method as for the chocolate favours, but using either milk or white chocolate. For some topping ideas see pages 248–9

Melt the chocolate in a heatproof bowl either over a pan of barely simmering water or in the microwave on a low setting. Remove from the heat, stir until smooth and leave to cool slightly.

Draw 10 x 5cm circles on the baking parchment, then flip the paper over so that it is pencil-side down on the baking tray. Spoon roughly one-third of the melted chocolate into a disposable piping bag and snip the end into a fine point. Pipe chocolate circles following the lines that you have drawn on the paper. Place a lolly stick in each circle so that the end sits at least 1cm into the middle of the lolly.

Pop the tray into the fridge for at least 10 minutes until set.

Spoon the remaining melted chocolate into the middle of each lolly in an even layer. Mix the chopped, toasted hazelnuts with the demerara sugar and orange zest and sprinkle over the chocolate lollies while they are still warm.

Refrigerate until set and then carefully peel off the paper to serve.

VANILLA BIRTHDAY CAKE

For me, a birthday cake is top of the bake list: you're celebrating the fact that the person in question is here on this earth with us, so let's make it special, something he or she really loves, whether it's simple or totally over the top. This is a classic vanilla: made with love, it can never fail to impress.

225g margarine or unsalted
   butter, softened
225g caster sugar
4 large eggs, beaten
1 tsp vanilla extract
225g self-raising flour
2 tbsp full-fat milk

Buttercream
500g icing sugar
125g unsalted butter, softened
3 tbsp full-fat milk
1 tsp vanilla extract

2 tbsp strawberry jam
sprinkles

You will also need 2 x 20cm
sandwich tins, greased and
the bases lined with buttered
baking parchment and
ribbons to decorate

Preheat the oven to 180°C/350°F/Gas Mark 4.

In the bowl of a free-standing mixer, cream the margarine or butter and sugar together until pale, light and fluffy. Gradually add the beaten eggs and vanilla extract. Add the flour and milk and mix until light and fluffy.

Divide equally between the prepared sandwich tins, spread level and bake on the middle shelf of the preheated oven for about 22–25 minutes until golden and a skewer comes away clean when inserted into the middle of the cakes.

Turn the cakes out of the tins onto a wire cooling rack and leave until cold.

To make the buttercream, tip all of the ingredients into the bowl of the free-standing mixer and beat until light and fluffy.

Lay one cake layer on a serving plate and spread with half of the buttercream. Top with strawberry jam. Spread the second cake layer with the remaining buttercream and finish with a circle of sprinkles around the outside edge, using your second hand as a guide to control the flow. Sandwich the two sponges together carefully and finish with a ribbon if you like.

CHOCOLATE BIRTHDAY CAKE

This little cake is such a simple show stopper. If the birthday girl or boy loves chocolate, a more perfect cake you won't find.

225g margarine or unsalted butter, softened
225g sugar
4 large eggs, beaten
1 tsp vanilla extract
200g self-raising flour
½ tsp baking powder
½ tsp bicarbonate of soda
30g cocoa
2 tbsp full-fat milk
100g good-quality dark chocolate, melted

Ganache
200g dark chocolate
100g milk chocolate
250ml double cream

Topping
1 large packet of Maltesers
sprinkles

You will also need 2 x 20cm sandwich tins, greased and the bases lined with buttered baking parchment, a piping bag fitted with a plain 1cm nozzle and ribbons to decorate

Preheat the oven to 180°C/350°F/Gas Mark 4.

In the bowl of a free-standing mixer, cream the margarine and sugar together until pale, light and fluffy. Gradually add the beaten eggs and vanilla extract. Add the flour, baking powder, bicarbonate of soda, cocoa and milk, then mix until combined. Add the melted chocolate and mix again until smooth.

Divide equally between the prepared sandwich tins, spread level and bake on the middle shelf of the preheated oven for about 22–25 minutes until golden and a skewer comes away clean when inserted into the middle of the cakes. Turn the cakes out of the tins onto a wire cooling rack and leave until cold.

To make the ganache, finely chop both the dark and milk chocolates and tip into a saucepan along with the double cream. Set the pan over a low heat to melt, stirring constantly until smooth. Pour the ganache into a shallow dish, cool and then chill to firm.

To assemble the cake, spoon half of the ganache into a piping bag fitted with a 1cm plain nozzle. Place one of the cake layers on a serving plate and, on the top of the cake, pipe a spiral of ganache starting from the outside and working into the middle. Scatter with a handful of lightly crushed Maltesers.

Cover the top of the second cake layer with ganache, spreading it smoothly with a palette knife. Sandwich the two cakes together and finish off with a good scattering of Maltesers and chocolate sprinkles.

EASTER BISCUITS

When I was a little girl I used to go with my nan to Devon, where we would stay at the farmhouse belonging to her friend, Rosa. She was an avid baker, so of course I was totally in my element. She would bake for all the men farmworkers in the family; they had this huge scrubbed pine table and a massive pantry. I remember being there and making these Easter biscuits with her. The dough is very soft and needs a really good chilling before cutting, but they are wonderful and exactly as I remember – so good, in fact that I don't just bake them at Easter.

250g unsalted butter, softened
130g caster sugar, plus extra
    for sprinkling
1 tsp vanilla extract
zest of half a lemon,
    finely grated
1 tbsp mixed peel paste
    (see pages 248–9)
1 large egg, beaten
300g plain flour, plus
    extra for dusting
1 egg white, beaten

You will also need a 6cm round fluted cutter and 2 baking trays lined with baking parchment

Preheat the oven to 180°C/350°F/Gas Mark 4.

Cream the butter and sugar together until pale, light and fluffy. Add the vanilla, lemon zest, mixed peel paste and egg, and mix again. Sieve the flour into the bowl and mix to bring the dough together. Turn out of the bowl, flatten into a disc, cover with cling film and leave the dough to chill in the fridge for 1 hour.

Dust a large piece of parchment with plain flour and place the dough on top. Cover with another piece of parchment and roll the dough out to a thickness of 3mm. Peel the top sheet of baking parchment off the dough and, using the cutter, stamp out round biscuits and place on prepared trays. Gather any dough scraps together, re-roll and stamp out more biscuits.

Bake on the middle shelf of the preheated oven for 10 minutes, then brush the biscuits with a little beaten egg white and sprinkle a little caster sugar. Return to the oven and bake for a further 5–7 minutes until golden.

Cool on wire racks.

SIMNEL CAKE

This is a fruit cake traditionally made at Easter, with eleven marzipan balls said to represent all the disciples (except Judas). When I was explaining this to Dylan, he looked at me in that sort of 'Mum, you're so simple' way and said, 'Eleven disciples? Do you know anything?'

300g mixed dried fruits
  (such as raisins, sultanas
  and currants)
150g unsalted butter, softened
75g soft light brown sugar
75g soft dark brown sugar
3 large eggs, beaten
200g self-raising flour
2 tsp mixed spice
40g mixed peel paste
  (see page 249)
20g crystallized or stem
  ginger, finely chopped
1 tbsp black treacle
3 tbsp apricot jam
400g marzipan

You will also need a 900g (2lb) loaf tin, greased and the base and ends lined with a strip of buttered baking parchment

Preheat the oven to 170°C/325°F/Gas Mark 3.

Soak the dried fruit for 10 minutes in a bowl of boiling water. Sieve and pat dry with kitchen paper.

Cream the butter and sugars together until light and fluffy. Gradually add the beaten eggs, mixing well between each addition. Using a large metal spoon, fold the flour and spice into the cake batter. Add the fruits, mixed peel, ginger and black treacle, and mix to thoroughly combine.

Roll 100g of the marzipan into a sausage the length of the tin, then flatten it into a rectangle with a rolling pin.

Spoon half the cake mixture into a prepared loaf tin and lay the marzipan on top. Cover with the rest of the cake mixture and spread level. Bake on the middle shelf of the oven for 1 hour, then turn the oven down to 150°C/300°F/Gas Mark 2 and bake for a further 50–60 minutes or until the cake is golden brown and a skewer inserted into the middle comes out clean.

Leave the cake to cool slightly in the tin, then turn out onto a wire rack to cool completely. Warm the apricot jam and sieve to remove any lumps. Brush the top of the cake with the jam.

Divide the remaining marzipan into two equal parts. Divide one piece into 11 even sized balls. Using the cake tin as a guide roll the remaining marzipan into a rectangle the same size as the top of the cake. Place the marzipan on top of the cake, score diamonds into the surface and top with the marzipan balls.

Place under the grill to gently colour the marzipan.

PRINCESS AND PIRATE CUPCAKES

These can be as hard or as simple as you'd like. If you're really creative, you can model eye patches and tiaras from sugarpaste, but if you don't feel up to them, sweeties are always a winner.

400g margarine or unsalted
   buetter, softened
400g caster sugar
6 large eggs, beaten
1 tsp vanilla extract
400g self-raising flour
3 tbsp full-fat milk

Buttercream
250g unsalted butter, softened
1 kg icing sugar
3 tbsp full-fat milk
2 gel colours (for example,
   black and pink)
assorted sprinkles and
   cupcake picks

Decoration
150g fondant and 150g
   gum paste combined to
   mould crowns and eye
   patches the day before
   and left to dry, optional.

You will also need 2 x 12-hole
muffin tins lined with paper
cases and two piping bags
fitted with large star nozzles

Preheat the oven to 170°C/325°F/Gas Mark 3.

In the bowl of a free-standing mixer, cream the margarine (or butter) and sugar together until light and fluffy.

Gradually add the beaten eggs mixing well between each addition. Add the vanilla extract. Sieve the flour into the bowl and mix again until the batter is smooth.

Divide the mixture between the 24 cupcake cases: bake on the middle shelf of the preheated oven for 20–25 minutes or until a wooden skewer inserted into the middle of the cakes comes out clean.

Leave to cool on a wire rack until cold before icing with buttercream.

To make the buttercream, beat the butter, icing sugar and milk together in a free-standing machine until light and fluffy. Take out a quarter of the buttercream and tint this black using the gel colour. Repeat with the pink gel.

Spoon half of the uncoloured buttercream into one side of a piping bag and spoon the pink or black into the other side. Pipe marbled buttercream swirls of pink or black onto the cupcakes.

Scatter with sprinkles and press a cupcake pick into the top of each cake to serve.

WEDDING TOWER

I think the idea of lots of little mini cakes is such a nice idea. I'm going to give the measurements for a three-layer topper and 15 mini cakes.

Topper
225g margarine or
  unsalted butter,
  softened
225g caster sugar
4 large eggs, beaten
1 tsp vanilla extract
225g self-raising flour
2 tbsp milk

Mini cakes
350g margarine or
  unsalted butter,
  softened
350g caster sugar
5 large eggs, beaten
2 tsp vanilla extract
350g self-raising flour
2–3 tbsp full-fat milk

Buttercream
2kg icing sugar, plus
  extra for rolling out
500g unsalted butter,
  softened
4–6 tbsp full-fat milk

Icing
2kg fondant or
  ready-to-roll icing

You will also need
3 x 18cm sandwich
cake tins, greased
and the bases lined
with buttered baking
parchment, and
15 x 6cm mini cake
tins, greased

Preheat the oven to 180°C/350°F/Gas Mark 4.

Make the cake topper first. In the bowl of a free-standing mixer, cream the margarine (or butter) and sugar together until pale, light and fluffy. Gradually add the beaten eggs and vanilla extract. Add the flour and milk, and mix until light and fluffy.

Divide equally between the 3 prepared sandwich tins, spread level and bake on the middle shelf of the preheated oven for about 20–25 minutes until golden and a skewer comes away clean when inserted into the middle of the cakes. Turn the cakes out of the tins onto a wire cooling rack and leave until cold.

Repeat the above method for the mini cakes, dividing the mixture evenly between the 15 prepared tins. Place on a baking tray and bake for 25–30 minutes. Cool on wire racks until cold.

To make the buttercream, tip all of the ingredients into the bowl of the free-standing mixer and beat until light and fluffy.

To assemble, place one of the 18cm cakes on a cake board and spread with buttercream, then top with the second cake and repeat this layering. Cover the whole 3-tier cake and the top and sides of each of the mini cakes with a thin layer of buttercream, spreading it evenly with a palette knife. Put into the freezer for 30 minutes to firm up.

Divide the fondant icing into 1 x 500g piece and 15 x 100g pieces. Dust the work surface with icing sugar and using a rolling pin roll one of the small pieces of icing at a time into a circle large enough to cover the top and sides of a mini cake. Lay the icing over the cake, smooth to cover and trim off any excess. Repeat with the remaining icing and cakes.

Roll the larger piece of icing into a disc large enough to cover the top and sides of the layer cake. Lay the icing over the cake and smooth the surface with your hands. Trim off any excess and leave all of the cakes to dry for 30 minutes.

To finish tie each cake in pretty ribbons and top with untreated roses with stalks covered in florists tape.

BAKING WITH CHILDREN

I think baking with children is such an important thing to do: not only is it a wonderful sharing experience but it's also an invaluable lesson for the future; it gives independence. An ability to bake is a wonderful skill, one that I'm eternally grateful to my nan and aunties for.

♥

PEANUT CORNFLAKE CAKES

These are so simple and quick to make. I think the added peanut butter gives an old favourite a new dimension.

40g unsalted butter
2tsp golden syrup
100g milk chocolate, chopped
2tsp peanut butter,
  crunchy or smooth
80g cornflakes
1 small bag of peanut M&Ms

You will also need
6 paper muffin cases
or 10 fairy cake cases

Combine the butter, golden syrup and milk chocolate in a saucepan over a low heat; stir until melted. Add the peanut butter and stir until smooth.

Tip the cornflakes into a large mixing bowl, pour over the chocolate mixture and stir until all of the cornflakes are coated.

Spoon the mixture into the paper cake cases and top with an M&M.

Chill in the fridge until set.

CHOCOLATE SMARTIE COOKIES

I think these little cookies are every child's dream, soft chocolatey cookies studded with everyone's favourite colourful sweetie.

200g unsalted butter, softened
300g soft brown sugar
2 large eggs
1 tsp vanilla extract
360g plain flour
40g cocoa
1 tsp bicarbonate of soda
pinch of salt
1tsp baking powder
200g smarties

You will also need a baking tray lined with baking parchment

Preheat the oven to 170°C/325°F/Gas Mark 3.

Mix the butter and sugar together in a free-standing machine until light and fluffy.

Beat the eggs and add them to the mixture a little at a time.

Scrape down the sides to make sure it is combined well and add vanilla extract.

Sift in the flour, cocoa, bicarb, salt and baking powder.

Mix until it reaches a clay like dough and fold in half the smarties.

With an ice-cream scoop or spoon put 10 cookie dough mounds onto the prepared trays.

Stud the cookie dough with the remaining smarties.

Bake for about 10 minutes on the middle shelf of the oven, taking them out half way through and giving a sharp bang on a work surface to knock out the air bubbles and flatten them.

Cool cookies slightly before transferring to wire racks to cool completely.

FAIRY CAKES

I still love fairy cakes: even now as a woman they still give me that same excitement as when I was a little girl going to a tea party. They are the first thing most children want to bake when they come to my kitchen.

175g caster sugar
175g margarine, softened
3 large eggs, beaten
175g self-raising flour
300g icing sugar
3–5 tbsp water, cold
assorted sweets and sprinkles

You will also need 2 bun trays lined with paper bun cases

Preheat the oven to 180°C/350°F/Gas Mark 4.

Cream the sugar and margarine together until pale, light and fluffy, either by hand or in a free-standing mixer.

Gradually add the eggs, mixing well between each addition and adding a teaspoon of the flour to the mixture if it starts to curdle.

Add the flour and mix until thoroughly combined.

Spoon the mixture into the paper bun cases, filling each one half full. Bake on the middle shelf of the oven for about 15–20 minutes until golden brown and well risen. A wooden skewer should come out clean when pushed into the cakes.

Remove the cakes from the bun tins and leave to cool on a wire rack.

Mix the icing sugar with enough water to make a thick paste.

Spoon the icing over the cooled fairy cakes; while the icing is still wet, decorate with assorted sweets and sprinkles.

ROCKY ROAD CUPCAKES

These fabulous-looking cupcakes have definitely got the wow factor: children and adults alike will love them.

40g unsalted butter or
    margarine, softened
140g caster sugar
120g self-raising flour
1 tsp baking powder
100ml full-fat milk
1 large egg, beaten
100g dark chocolate, melted

Rocky road toppers
100g milk chocolate
1 handful of mini marshmallows
1 handful of popcorn
50g white chocolate

Marshmallow buttercream
70g marshmallows
3 tsp double cream
100g unsalted butter, softened
500g icing sugar
3 tbsp full-fat milk

**You will also need a muffin
tin lined with 8–10 paper
muffin cases and a baking
tray lined with parchment
and a piping bag with a
large nozzle**

Preheat the oven to 170°C/325°F/Gas Mark 3.

Combine the butter, caster sugar, flour and baking powder in the bowl of a free-standing mixer and mix until you have a sandy texture. Add 50ml of milk and whisk until well combined.

Add the remaining milk, egg and cooled melted chocolate to the batter and mix thoroughly.

Divide the mixture evenly between the muffin cases filling them two-thirds full. Bake on the middle shelf of the oven for 20–25 minutes or until well risen and a wooden skewer comes out clean when inserted. Cool on a wire rack before decorating.

To make the toppers, pop the baking tray into the freezer for 10 minutes to chill.

Melt the milk chocolate and pour a thin layer onto the chilled baking tray. Scatter over the mini marshmallows and popcorn.

Melt the white chocolate and, using a teaspoon, drizzle it over the rocky road. Pop the tray back into the freezer to set for about 5 minutes.

To make the buttercream, heat the marshmallows and cream in a small saucepan until melted.

Beat the softened butter, icing sugar and milk together in a free-standing machine until smooth. Add the melted marshmallows and beat again until light and fluffy, this will take about 5 minutes.

Spoon the buttercream into the piping bag and pipe swirls onto each cooled cupcake. Break the rocky road into pieces and press into the buttercream to serve.

LITTLE HARLEY AND HENRY HEDGEHOG ROLLS

These are the sort of bakes I love to make with my godchildren and look forward to making with Harley when he is a little bigger. I would probably make the dough in advance, though, because children can be really impatient waiting for it to prove.

300g strong white bread flour
½ tsp sea salt
4g (1 tsp) caster sugar
4g (1 tsp) easy-blend/fast-action yeast
100ml water, warmed
50ml full-fat milk, warmed
10g unsalted butter, softened
20 currants
5 glacé cherries, quartered
1 large egg, beaten

You will also need 2 baking trays

Tip the flour, salt, sugar and yeast either into the bowl of a free-standing mixer fitted with a bread hook or into a large bowl, and mix until combined. Make a well in the middle of the dry ingredients.

Combine the warm water and milk in a jug, add the softened butter and stir so that the butter starts to melt. Slowly pour the warm liquid into the dry ingredients and mix until combined.

Knead for about 7 minutes in the mixer or for 10–12 minutes by hand (little hands may need some help here) until smooth and soft.

Put the dough into a lightly greased mixing bowl, cover with cling film and leave to prove until doubled in size. This will take about 1–1½ hours.

Turn out onto the work surface and knead for about 1 minute to knock back the dough. Divide evenly into 10 balls and form pinecone-shaped rolls. Place 5 rolls on each baking tray, then cover with greased cling film and leave to prove for 1 hour.

Preheat the oven to 200°C/400°F/Gas Mark 6.

Push currant eyes into each roll and a cherry quarter for his nose. Brush each roll with beaten egg.

Use scissors to snip little spikes onto each roll. Bake in the middle of the oven for 12–15 minutes until they sound hollow when tapped underneath.

Cool on wire racks before serving.

Baking with children

BANANA MUFFINS

These are really lovely and simple to make with children, who love rubbing and sprinkling the crumbly topping. With the addition of banana, they're a great packed-lunch treat.

280g self-raising flour
½ tsp bicarbonate of soda
½ tsp baking powder
180g caster sugar
2 bananas
300ml buttermilk
90g unsalted butter, melted
1 large egg

Toppings
60g plain flour
50g unsalted butter,
    chilled and diced
20g demerara sugar
1 tsp ground cinnamon
1 tsp orange zest, finely grated
100g pecans, finely chopped
    (optional)

You will also need a
12-hole muffin tin lined
with paper cases

Preheat the oven to 190°C/375°F/Gas Mark 5.

Make the topping first. In a small bowl, rub together the flour, butter, sugar, cinnamon and orange zest until the mixture is crumbly and the butter is completely incorporated. Add the chopped pecans if using.

To make the muffins, combine the flour, bicarbonate of soda, baking powder and caster sugar in a large bowl and make a well in the centre.

In another bowl, mash the bananas with a fork.

In a jug, whisk together the buttermilk, melted butter and egg.

Add the mashed banana and wet ingredients into the well in the dry ingredients and fold together using a large metal spoon until only just combined. Do not overwork the mixture as the muffins will become tough and heavy.

Divide the mixture between the muffin cases and sprinkle the top of each muffin with the crumbly topping. Bake on the middle shelf of the preheated oven for 30 minutes until well risen, golden brown and a skewer inserted into the middle of a muffin comes out clean.

Cool slightly on a wire rack before serving warm or at room temperature.

MINI PIZZAS

These are quick and easy and children just love them. They also really encourage fussy eaters to try new things and are a fab idea for children's parties.

Dough
300g self-raising flour,
    plus extra for kneading
300g Greek yoghurt
1 tsp baking powder
1 tsp salt
12 tbsp passata or
    barbecue sauce
dried herbs (such as
    oregano, optional)
180g mozzarella, drained
    and torn into small pieces
120g cheddar cheese, grated
olive oil

Extra topping ideas
ham or Prosciutto, chopped
chicken breast, cooked
    and shredded
pepperoni slices
roasted peppers
cherry tomatoes, halved
sweetcorn
button mushrooms, sliced
rocket

You will also need
2 large baking trays

Preheat the oven to 200°C/400°F/Gas Mark 6.

Tip the flour, Greek yoghurt, baking powder and salt into a food processor and mix until combined and smooth. Turn the dough out onto a lightly floured work surface and knead for 30 seconds.

Divide the dough into 6 equal pieces and roll into discs roughly the size of a saucer.

Pop two baking trays in the hot oven to preheat.

Spread 2 tablespoons of tomato passata or barbecue sauce on top of each pizza base and sprinkle with a pinch of dried herbs if using. Scatter the mozzarella and cheddar evenly over the pizza bases and top with a combination of the extra toppings.

Take the hot baking trays out of the oven and quickly brush with a little oil.

Put 2 pizzas onto each hot baking tray and cook in the hot oven for 8–12 minutes until golden and bubbling. Repeat with the remaining 2 pizzas. Serve immediately.

CHEWY FRUITY FLAPJACKS

Flapjacks always remind me of my brother Mark and the first time I ever made them. It was in a home economics class when I was about thirteen so Mark would have been twelve. He loved them so much he nearly ate the whole trayful. I know I've said it before, but that's what I so love about baking: memories of loved ones and happy times shared.

250g unsalted butter
175g soft light brown sugar
150g golden syrup
300g rolled oats
150g dried apricots, chopped
100g dried cranberries

You will also need a 20cm square baking tin lined with either a reusable liner or non-stick baking parchment

Preheat the oven to 150°C/300°F/Gas Mark 3.

In a large saucepan, melt the butter, sugar and syrup together over a gentle heat.

Once everything has melted, remove the pan from the heat, pour in the oats, chopped dried apricots and cranberries, and stir well with a wooden spoon.

Transfer the mixture into the prepared tin and spread level.

Bake on the middle shelf of the preheated oven for 20 minutes until golden brown and starting to firm at the edges.

Remove from the oven and, using a sharp knife, mark out slices while the flapjack is still hot.

Leave the flapjack until completely cold before serving.

JAM TARTS

I know these are simple but for me this is where it all started. My Nanny Billie was a massive influence on me when it comes to baking. Most weekends as a little girl were spent in my nan's home, and she would play shops with me. I, of course, would be the shopkeeper, having the contents of her whole larder over the kitchen table, and she would always play the long-suffering customer. When we weren't playing shop or watching Hawaii Five-O *we would be baking, and with my nan it was always pastry. That's where the jam tarts first came in – I'd always have the offcuts and a jar of Robertson's jam… that's how my love of baking was born.*

**150g plain flour, plus
   extra for rolling out
75g unsalted butter,
   chilled and diced
60g icing sugar
1 large egg yolk
1–3 tbsp full-fat milk
assorted jams**

**You will also need a
12-hole patty/bun tin
and a 7.5cm fluted cutter**

In a food processor combine the flour, butter, and icing sugar using the pulse button until the mixture is crumbly and sand-like. Add the egg yolk and the milk, one tablespoon at a time, until your pastry starts to come together.

Turn the pastry out onto the work surface and knead for 30 seconds, flatten into a disc, wrap in cling film and chill for 30 minutes.

Preheat the oven to 180°C/350°F/Gas Mark 4.

Lightly flour the work surface and roll the pastry to a thickness of 3–4mm and cut into rounds using a pastry cutter. Press the pastry discs into the patty tins and spoon one teaspoonful of jam into each. Chill the tarts for 10 minutes and then bake on the middle shelf of the preheated oven for 15 minutes until the pastry is pale golden.

Leave the jam tarts to firm up in the patty tins for 5 minutes and then transfer onto a wire cooling rack until cold.

SHAPED AND ICED COOKIES

Children love making these cookies. Many will remember the fun they had for the rest of their lives, and it's a unique thrill for an adult to watch such memories in the making.

250g plain flour, plus
 extra for rolling out
1 tsp baking powder
80g caster sugar
110g unsalted butter,
 diced and chilled
1 large egg, beaten
1 tsp vanilla extract
1 x 500g packet of royal
 icing sugar
gel food colours

**You will also need cookie
cutters in assorted shapes
and parchment-covered
baking trays**

In a food processor mix the flour, baking powder and sugar until combined. Add the butter and pulse again until incorporated. Add the egg and vanilla extract and pulse again until the dough is smooth. Turn out onto the work surface and bring together into a ball. Flatten into a disc, cover with cling film and chill for 30 minutes.

Lightly flour the work surface and roll the dough out to the thickness of a £1 coin. Using cutters, stamp out shapes and arrange on the parchment-lined baking trays. Gather any dough scraps together, re-roll and stamp out more cookies. Chill on the baking trays in the freezer for 20 minutes.

Meanwhile preheat the oven to 190°C/375°F/Gas Mark 5.

Bake the cookies on the middle shelf of the oven for 10–15 minutes until golden, leave to firm and cool slightly on baking trays and then transfer to wire racks until cold.

Make up the royal icing as instructed on the pack. Spoon 3–4 tablespoons of icing into a disposable piping bag and snip the end into a fine nozzle. Pipe outlines around all of the cookies and leave to dry for 15 minutes.

Add a drop more water to the remaining icing so that it is slightly runnier than that used for the outlines. Use gel food colours to tint the icing whatever colour you choose. Carefully spoon the icing onto each cookie so that it fills the outline evenly. Leave the icing to dry for a good few hours or even overnight.

Chapter seven

BREADS

I have such a passion for making bread that until really recently I'd only ever used the bread hook on my free-standing machine. But then I was shown the joy of kneading by hand and I discovered that it almost connects you with the dough: it gives you a real feel for the amount of elasticity that you have achieved. I know it can be time-consuming but it can also be a means of relaxation – we are all normally in such a hurry that sometimes it's nice to give ourselves a break, a little time out to do something for ourselves and ultimately produce a nourishing gift for our loved ones. No two kitchens are the same, and slight temperature variations from one to another can significantly affect the proving time of your bake. One great tip is to use those plastic storage boxes that create a fantastic proving environment; another is to ensure that all your ingredients are at room temperature before starting to bake.

SODA BREAD

I thought I'd start with a nice easy loaf. I adore this simple bread, and when it's no longer at its freshest it is fabulous toasted with lashings of butter and jam, but best of all toasted with crispy bacon.

450g plain flour, plus
 extra for dusting
1 tsp caster sugar
1 ½ tsp bicarbonate of soda
1 ½ tsp salt
300ml buttermilk
100ml full-fat milk
1 tbsp lemon juice

**You will also need
a solid baking tray**

Preheat the oven to 220°C/425°F/Gas Mark 7.

Sift all the dry ingredients into a large bowl, combine and make a well in the centre.

Mix the buttermilk, milk and lemon juice in a jug.

Pour the wet ingredients into the flour, and mix together using a wooden spoon or spatula until the dough starts to come together.

Lightly dust the work surface with a little plain flour; tip the dough out of the bowl and lightly knead to just bring the dough into a round loaf. Do not overwork the dough as this will result in tough bread.

Place the loaf on the baking tray and, using a knife, score a cross in the top.

Reduce the oven temperature to 200°C/400°F/Gas Mark 6 and bake the soda bread on the middle shelf for about 25–30 minutes until the loaf is well risen, golden and will sound hollow when tapped on the bottom.

PLAITED ENRICHED WHITE LOAF

A restaurant where we sometimes go has these amazing little rolls that are soft and light and almost sweet. I know it's strange but I could almost go there just for them. I don't think the restaurateur would be too pleased if I did, but luckily the rest of the menu is fab as well.

250g strong plain bread flour, plus extra for kneading
7g easy-blend/fast-action yeast
2 tsp caster sugar
5g salt
25g unsalted butter, softened
100ml full-fat milk
50ml water
1 egg, beaten with 1 tbsp water

Preheat the oven to 210°C/410°F/Gas Mark 6.

In a large bowl, place the flour, yeast, sugar and salt, then make a well in the centre.

Combine the water and milk and heat to lukewarm.

Mix the softened butter into the warm fluid until it starts to dissolve.

Pour into the dry ingredients and knead for 6 minutes on a bread hook or 10 minutes by hand.

Put into an oiled bowl; cover and leave to double in size (this will take about 1 hour). Turn out onto a floured surface; knock back and knead for 2 more minutes.

Divide into 3 equal pieces and roll into 20cm sausage shapes.

Plait as though you were braiding hair.

Put onto a baking tray, cover and leave to prove for 1 hour.

Brush with an egg wash and maybe sprinkle on some poppy or sesame seeds.

Bake in the oven for about 25–30 minutes or until it sounds hollow when tapped underneath.

Cool on a wire rack.

BASIC GRANARY BREAD

This is another really simple recipe. You could add a handful of seeds in with the dry ingredients if you'd like to give it another dimension. It's fantastic when fresh, but also great toasted when it's past its best.

200g strong bread flour,
 plus extra for kneading
300g granary bread flour
8g salt
1 tbsp caster sugar
7g easy-blend/fast-action yeast
100ml full-fat milk
200ml water
1 tbsp sunflower oil
1 egg yolk, beaten
20g pumpkin seeds

You will also need a 900g (2lb) loaf tin, lightly greased

Bits & Bobs

Flavoured butter
For a little extra 'oomph' it's nice to soften some unsalted butter in a bowl and mix through a complementary flavour to serve with your main dish. This could be used to top fish, spread on some home-made bread, or to add interest to vegetables. See pages 248-9.

Tip all the dry ingredients except the pumpkin seeds into the bowl of a free-standing machine fitted with the bread hook attachment, or into a large mixing bowl, and make a well in the centre.

Heat the milk and water together until lukewarm. Add the sunflower oil and stir to combine.

Combine with dry ingredients and, with the machine running on a slow to medium speed, mix until the dough comes together – you may not need all of the liquid. If mixing by hand, just use a wooden spoon or spatula. Continue to knead in the machine for 7 minutes or by hand for about 10–12 minutes until you have a smooth, elastic dough.

Shape into a ball and place in a large, lightly oiled bowl; cover with cling film and leave in a warm place for about 1–1½ hours or until doubled in size.

Tip out onto a floured work surface and knead for 1 minute to knock back the dough. Mould it into a sausage shape and pop into the loaf tin. Cover with oiled cling film and leave to prove for 40–60 minutes until the dough has doubled in size and feels springy.

Preheat the oven to 200°C/400°F/Gas Mark 6.

Gently brush the top of the loaf or rolls with the beaten egg yolk and scatter with pumpkin seeds.

Bake just below the middle of the oven for 30–35 minutes or until golden brown and the underside sounds hollow when tapped.

Cool the loaf in the tin for 10 minutes and then turn out onto a wire rack and leave until cold before slicing.

BASIC WHITE LOAF

I adore white bread. It really doesn't like me, but that's no deterrent. I love nothing better at the moment than two slices of home-made white, generously smeared with a good mayo, a big dollop of cranberry sauce and some slices of turkey breast: my idea of heaven; my mouth is watering just writing about it!

500g strong white bread flour, plus extra for kneading
8g sea salt
8g caster sugar
7g easy-blend/fast-action yeast
100ml full-fat milk
200ml water
25g unsalted butter, melted
1 egg yolk, beaten

You will also need a 900g (2lb) loaf tin, lightly greased

Bits & Bobs

Canapés
To make lovely, easy little canapé bases, you can use a medium pastry cutter to stamp out circles from 2–3 day-old sliced bread. For topping ideas see pages 248–9.

Tip all the dry ingredients into the bowl of a free-standing machine fitted with a bread hook or into a large mixing bowl, and make a well in the centre.

Heat the milk and water together until lukewarm. Add the melted butter and stir to combine.

Combine with the dry ingredients and, with the machine running on a slow to medium speed, mix until the dough comes together. Alternatively, if mixing by hand, just use a wooden spoon or spatula. Continue to knead in the machine for 7 minutes or by hand for about 10–12 minutes until you have a smooth, elastic dough.

Shape the dough into a ball and place in a large, lightly oiled bowl; cover with cling film and leave in a warm place for about 1 hour or until doubled in size.

Tip out onto a lightly floured work surface and knead for 1 minute to knock back the dough. Mould it into a sausage shape and pop into the loaf tin, cover with oiled cling film and leave to prove for 40–60 minutes until the dough has doubled in size and feels springy.

Preheat the oven to 200°C/400°F/Gas Mark 6.

Gently brush the top of the loaf with the beaten egg yolk and bake just below the middle of the preheated oven for 30 minutes until golden brown and the underside of the loaf sounds hollow when tapped.

Cool the loaf in the tin for 10 minutes and then turn out onto a wire rack and leave until cold before slicing.

CINNAMON AND SUGAR SWIRL LOAF

This loaf puts me in mind of all things homely: I think cinnamon tends to do that.

350g plain flour, plus extra for kneading
350g strong plain flour
14g easy-blend/fast-action yeast
50g caster sugar
1 tbsp salt
200ml full-fat milk
50ml water
30g unsalted butter, softened
2 large eggs, beaten
1 tbsp ground cinnamon
30g demerara sugar
20g unsalted butter, melted
1 egg, beaten with 1 tbsp water

You will also need
2 x 900g (2lb) loaf tins, lightly greased

Tip the flours, yeast, caster sugar and salt into the bowl of a free-standing mixer fitted with a dough hook or a large mixing bowl, and make a well in the centre.

Heat the milk and water together until lukewarm. Add the butter, stir until melted and then add the beaten eggs. Pour into the dry ingredients and mix until you have a soft dough. Continue to knead for 7 minutes using the dough hook or for 10 minutes by hand until the dough is smooth and elastic. Shape into a ball and place in an oiled bowl; cover with cling film and leave in a warm place to prove for 90 minutes or until doubled in size.

Turn out onto a floured work surface and knead for 1 minute to knock back. Split into two 25 x 35cm rectangles, roughly 1cm thick.

Mix together the cinnamon and demerara sugar. Brush each dough rectangle with melted butter and sprinkle with the cinnamon sugar.

Fold the longer ends of each rectangle over by 1–2cm and then roll the dough into a tight spiral, starting with the shorter end. Pop one roll into each tin, cover with oiled cling film and leave to prove for 1 hour or until doubled in size and springy.

Preheat the oven to 200°C/400°F/Gas Mark 6.

Brush the top of each loaf with beaten egg and bake just below the middle shelf of the oven for about 25 minutes until well-risen and golden brown. Take the loaves out of the tins, turn upside down and return to the oven for a further 5 minutes to brown the undersides.

Cool on wire racks before slicing.

STROMBOLI

This is one of Dylan's favourites: it's such a fantastic picnic loaf, almost like a modern-day pasty with the flavours of the Continent in it.

1 jar of roasted peppers
   in olive oil
2 handfuls of fresh basil leaves
340g strong white flour, plus
   extra for kneading
7g easy-blend/fast-action yeast
1 tsp caster sugar
1 tsp salt
200ml water, warmed
100g sun-dried tomatoes,
   drained
150g mozzarella (not buffalo),
   drained
4 sprigs of rosemary

You will also need
a large baking tray

Drain the peppers and reserve the oil. Pour 2 tablespoons of the oil and half of the basil leaves into a pestle and mortar and pound until lightly crushed and bruised. Leave for 30 minutes to infuse.

Combine the flour, yeast, sugar and salt in a mixing bowl and make a well in the centre. Strain the basil-infused oil into the flour, then slowly add 200ml of the water and mix until you have a soft dough. Knead either by hand for 10 minutes or in a free-standing mixer fitted with a dough hook for 6 minutes. Once the dough is smooth and elastic, place in a large, oiled bowl. Cover with cling film and leave in a warm place for about 1 hour or until doubled in size.

Turn out onto a floured work surface and knead for 1 minute to knock back and then roll into a 40 x 20cm rectangle. Brush with 1 tablespoon of the oil, then scatter the remaining basil leaves, roasted peppers and sun-dried tomatoes on top. Tear the mozzarella into pieces and scatter evenly over the dough.

Fold the shorter ends of the rectangle over and roll the dough into a tight Swiss roll spiral. Carefully transfer the roll to the tray with the seam on the underside. Cover with oiled cling film and leave to prove for 1 hour or until doubled in size.

Preheat the oven to 220°C/425°F/Gas Mark 7.

Brush the loaf with the oil and push the rosemary sprigs into the top. Bake in the middle of the oven for 30 minutes until golden brown, turning the temperature down to 200°C/400°F/Gas Mark 6 after 10 minutes.

Cool and then cut into thick slices to serve.

SPICED ORANGE ROLLS

I first made these for my stepmum Shelly and her mum Kath, who said they made their mouths water: they're almost juicy. I know that sounds strange for bread, but when you try them I think you'll agree.

625g strong white flour,
    plus extra for kneading
7g easy-blend/fast-action yeast
60g caster sugar
½ tsp salt
250ml full-fat milk
100ml orange juice, freshly
    squeezed
30g unsalted butter, melted
1 large egg, beaten
zest of 2 oranges, grated

Filling
25g unsalted butter, melted
60g demerara sugar
1 tsp ground mixed spice
1 tsp ground cinnamon
60g pecans, finely chopped
zest of 1 orange, grated

Icing
juice of half an orange
100g icing sugar

You will also need a 12-hole
muffin tin, lightly buttered

Tip the flour into a large mixing bowl; add the yeast, sugar and salt and make a well in the centre. Heat the milk until lukewarm, add the orange juice, melted butter, beaten egg and grated orange zest, and mix to combine.

Gradually pour into the dry ingredients and mix until you have a soft dough. Knead in a free-standing mixer fitted with a dough hook for 6 minutes or by hand for 10 minutes until the dough is smooth and elastic.

Shape into a ball and place in an oiled mixing bowl. Cover with cling film and leave in a warm place for about 1 hour or until doubled in size.

Turn out onto a floured work surface and knead for 1 minute to knock back. Roll into a large, neat rectangle 1cm thick and brush liberally with the melted butter. In a small bowl, mix together the sugar, spices, nuts and orange zest and sprinkle over the dough.

With the long side of the rectangle nearest to you, roll the dough away from you into a tight spiral. Brush with a little melted butter to seal the roll. Trim off the ends and slice the roll into 12 equal portions. Pop the buns into the buttered muffin tin, cut-side uppermost. Cover with oiled cling film and leave to prove for 40 minutes or until doubled in size.

Preheat the oven to 200°C/400°F/Gas Mark 6.

Bake the rolls on the middle shelf of the oven for 20–25 minutes until well risen and golden brown.

Cool for 10–15 minutes in the tin. Meanwhile, whisk together the orange juice and the icing sugar and drizzle over the buns and leave to set before serving.

RASPBERRY ICED FINGERS

These are such pretty iced buns – they would work fabulously for a girly tea party. You can always divide the buns in two at the shaping stage and make 20 mini ones.

400g strong white flour,
    plus extra for kneading
100g plain flour
10g easy-blend/fast-
    action yeast
50g caster sugar
1½ tsp salt
300ml full-fat milk, warmed
60g unsalted butter, softened

Toppings and fillings
5 tbsp raspberry jam
600ml double cream
20 fresh raspberries
200g icing sugar

You will also need 2 baking trays and a piping bag fitted with a large star nozzle

Combine both of the flours, yeast, sugar and salt in a large mixing bowl. Add the butter and mix to combine. Make a well in the centre of the dry ingredients, add the milk and butter, and mix to a soft dough. Knead on a floured surface for 5 minutes until smooth and elastic, then shape into a ball and pop into an oiled mixing bowl. Cover with cling film and leave in a warm place to prove for 1 hour or until doubled in size.

Turn out onto a floured surface and knead for 1 minute to knock back. Divide the dough into 10 evenly sized pieces.

Roll each piece into a sausage shape roughly 15cm long and arrange onto 2 baking trays, spacing well apart to allow them to spread during proving and baking. Cover with oiled cling film and leave to prove for 40 minutes or until springy.

Preheat the oven to 200°C/400°F/Gas Mark 6.

Bake the buns on the middle shelf of the oven for 30 minutes until golden. Transfer to wire racks to cool.

To finish, warm the jam and sieve to remove the seeds. Whip the double cream until it will just hold stiff peaks and spoon into a piping bag. Push the raspberries through a sieve to remove the seeds. Mix with the icing sugar until stiff but spreadable, adding more sugar if needed.

Split the buns through the middle and spread the bottom half of each with the sieved raspberry jam. Top with whipped cream. Using a palette knife, spread the top of each bun with raspberry icing. Leave to set before serving.

SUNFLOWER SEED ROLLS

These are fab little dinner rolls that work really well in terracotta plant pots: I just get regular little pots from the garden centre, oiled and baked twice before using. They look so cute when you're having a barbecue, almost like a little edible centrepiece.

**170g strong white flour,
  plus extra for kneading**
170g strong wholemeal flour
**7g easy-blend/fast-
  action yeast**
1 tsp salt
275ml buttermilk
1 tbsp clear honey
50ml sunflower oil
100g sunflower seeds
1 tbsp full-fat milk

**You will also need a
12-hole muffin tin or
12 small terracotta pots,
lightly oiled**

Tip both of the flours into a large mixing bowl, add the yeast and salt, mix to combine and make a well in the centre. Warm the buttermilk in a small pan until lukewarm, then add the honey and sunflower oil and mix to combine. Pour into the well in the dry ingredients and mix to a soft dough. Knead the dough either in a free-standing mixer fitted with a dough hook for 6 minutes or by hand for 10 minutes. Once the dough is smooth and elastic, add 75g of the sunflower seeds and knead again until thoroughly combined.

Shape the dough into a ball and place in a large mixing bowl; cover with cling film and leave in a warm place for about 1 hour or until doubled in size.

Turn out onto a lightly floured work surface and knead again for 1 minute to knock back. Divide into 12 even pieces, shape into neat balls and place either in the muffin tins or the terracotta pots. Cover with oiled cling film and leave for another hour until well risen and springy.

Preheat the oven to 200°C/400°F/Gas Mark 6.

Gently brush the rolls with milk, sprinkle with the remaining sunflower seeds and bake on the middle shelf of the preheated oven for 15–20 minutes until golden brown and well risen. Remove from tins and cool on wire racks.

HALLOUMI AND CHILLI FLAKE FLATBREADS

These are wonderful if, like me, yeast isn't your best friend. They are also the quickest breads I've found and are so versatile. I've given the recipe here for halloumi and chilli but you could use any number of different flavours. They are excellent as wraps and fantastic with curry. You could also use them to make chicken fajitas. With only six ingredients, three of which you'll always have in the cupboard, you can make these on a whim.

300g self-raising flour, plus extra for kneading
1 tsp baking powder
1 tsp salt
300g Greek yoghurt
1 tbsp crushed dried chilli flakes
80g halloumi, crumbled
chilli-infused oil

You will also need a flat (smooth) griddle pan or large, solid-based frying pan

Tip the flour, baking powder and salt into the bowl of the food processor. Add the Greek yoghurt and chilli flakes and whizz until the dough comes together.

Turn the dough out onto a lightly floured work surface and knead until smooth. Mix the crumbled halloumi into the dough and then divide into 8 equal pieces. Roll each piece of dough out into a disc roughly the size of a saucer.

Place the griddle or frying pan over a medium heat, brush with a little chilli oil and cook the flatbreads 1 at a time for about 1–2 minutes on each side until golden brown.

Chapter eight

BISCUITS AND COOKIES

*What in the world could be better than a good cup
of tea and some lovely buttery home-made biscuits,
which are so much better than anything you'll buy.
I find them one of the easiest bakes, a perfect job for
a novice. I use an ice cream scoop to measure my
cookie dough as I find it gives uniform-sized bakes
at room temperature before starting to bake.*

♥

PEANUT BUTTER COOKIES

These are a massive favourite in my house. My sister-in-law Sonia introduced me to them more years ago than I care to remember. I always have a jar of peanut butter in the house, so I'm only ever 20 minutes away from a lovely crumbly cookie.

100g unsalted butter, softened

100g peanut butter, either smooth or crunchy

60g demerara sugar

60g caster sugar

1 large egg, beaten

100g plain flour

½ tsp baking powder

½ tsp bicarbonate of soda

60g salted peanuts or chocolate chips

You will also need 2–3 baking trays covered with baking parchment

Preheat the oven to 180°C/350°F/Gas Mark 4.

Cream the butter, peanut butter, demerara and caster sugar in a free-standing mixer until pale, light and fluffy.

Gradually add the egg and mix until thoroughly combined.

Sift the flour, baking powder and bicarbonate of soda into the bowl and mix until smooth and the dough comes together. Add the peanuts or chocolate chips.

Scoop the dough onto the prepared baking trays using either an ice-cream scoop or a large spoon, allowing plenty of space between each cookie as they will spread during cooking. Bake in batches on the middle shelf of the preheated oven for 5 minutes and then take the tray out of the oven and give it a sharp bang on the work surface to deflate the cookies. Return to the oven for a further 5 minutes until golden brown.

Cool slightly on the trays before transferring the cookies to wire racks until cold.

Bits & Bobs

Hot chocolate
I love 'real' hot chocolate. I've never been skiing, but I imagine the hot chocolate that everyone talks about is rich, sweet and creamy! See pages 248–9 for my version.

OAT AND RAISIN COOKIES

These are really yummy oaty, fruity biscuits. I love anything with oats as it gives you a great slow release of energy throughout the day.

170g unsalted butter, softened
200g soft light brown sugar
120g caster sugar
1 large egg, beaten
4 tsp sunflower oil
250g plain flour
½ tsp bicarbonate of soda
½ tsp cinnamon
150g rolled oats
200g raisins

You will also need 2–3 baking trays lined with baking parchment

Preheat the oven to 180°C/350°F/Gas Mark 4.

In the bowl of a free-standing mixer, cream together the butter and both of the sugars until pale and light. Add the egg and oil and mix again.

Sift the flour, bicarbonate of soda and cinnamon into the bowl, add the oats and raisins and mix again until smooth and thoroughly combined.

Using your hands, roll the cookie dough into walnut-sized balls and place onto the prepared baking trays. Allow plenty of space between each cookie as they will spread during baking.

Slightly flatten the cookies with the palm of your hand and bake on the middle shelf of the preheated oven for about 20 minutes until pale golden and firm.

Cool on wire racks.

CHOCOLATE CHIP COOKIES

There was a time when I was forever knocking up batch after batch of chocolate chip cookies to feed my three boys and the starving hordes they brought home with them. They're easy to make from ingredients that I've nearly always got in my store cupboard and they take no time at all.

200g unsalted butter, softened
200g light soft brown sugar
125g demerara sugar
2 large eggs, beaten
1 tsp vanilla extract
400g plain flour
1 tsp baking powder
1 tsp bicarbonate of soda
a pinch of salt
200g dark chocolate chunks
   (I like hand-cut)

You will also need 2–3 baking trays covered with baking parchment

Preheat the oven to 170°C/325°F/Gas Mark 3.

Cream the butter and both of the sugars together in a free-standing machine until pale, light and fluffy.

Gradually add the beaten eggs, mixing well between each addition. Scrape down the sides of the bowl with a rubber spatula, add the vanilla extract and mix again.

Sift the flour, baking powder, bicarbonate of soda and a pinch of salt into the bowl and mix again until thoroughly combined. Fold the chocolate chunks into the cookie dough.

Use either an ice-cream scoop or large spoon to scoop the dough into even-sized mounds. Place 3–4 cookies on each baking tray, allowing plenty of space between each cookie as they will spread during cooking.

Bake the cookies in batches on the middle shelf of the preheated oven for about 5 minutes. Remove from the oven and sharply bang the baking tray on the work surface to deflate the cookies, then return to the oven for a further 5–7 minutes until pale golden brown.

Allow the cookies to cool on the baking trays for a few minutes before transferring to wire racks until cold.

PISTACHIO AND ORANGE SHORTBREAD HEARTS

These two flavours work so well together, and when combined with the gorgeous texture of the shortbread you honestly can't go wrong. They're perfect for afternoon tea on the lawn or with a cuppa in the kitchen.

60g unsalted pistachios, shelled
225g unsalted butter, softened
100g caster sugar, plus extra
**   for sprinkling**
225g plain flour, plus extra
**   for dusting**
60g semolina
zest of 1 orange, finely grated

You will also need 2 baking trays lined with baking parchment and heart-shaped cookie cutters

Whizz the pistachios in the food processor until finely chopped and tip into a bowl. Add the butter, caster sugar, flour and semolina, and using your fingers rub the butter into the dry ingredients. Add the grated orange zest and work until the mixture comes together.

Turn the dough out onto a lightly floured work surface and knead very gently until smooth. Shape the dough into a ball, flatten into a disc, wrap in cling film and chill in the fridge for 30 minutes.

Lightly dust the work surface with flour and roll the dough out to a thickness of about 4mm. Using heart-shaped cutters, stamp out cookies and arrange on lined baking trays. Gather any dough off cuts into a ball and re-roll to make more cookies. Chill the cookies for a further 30 minutes.

Meanwhile preheat the oven 170°C/325°F/ Gas Mark 3.

Bake the cookies on the middle shelf of the oven for about 15–18 minutes or until very pale golden.

Remove from the oven, sprinkle with caster sugar and then transfer to wire racks to cool.

CRYSTALLISED GINGER BISCUITS

When I quizzed my team of biscuit tasters to discover which flavour they preferred, an overwhelming majority plumped for ginger. I'm assured that mine are winners - crunchy on the outside and soft on the inside, with a mention of dark or white chocolate adorning the top. I can't comment because ginger really doesn't like me very much!

90g unsalted butter, softened
110g demerara sugar
40g light muscavodo sugar
250g plain flour
1 tsp ground ginger
1 tsp ground cinnamon
1 tsp flavourless oil
   (sunflower or groundnut)
75g crystallised ginger,
   chopped
10 squares of dark or
   white chocolate

**You will also need 2 baking trays
lined with baking parchment**

Preheat oven to 180°C/350°F/Gas Mark 4.

Cream the butter with the demerara and light muscovado sugars in the food processor until light and fluffy.

Sift the flour, ground ginger and cinnamon into the bowl and mix again. Add oil and ginger and process until combined.

Using a teaspoon, scoop a small mound of dough into your hand and roll into a ball. Place on a lined baking tray and flatten slightly with the palm of your hand. Repeat with the remaining dough.

Cut each chocolate square in half and push one piece into the top of each biscuit.

Bake the ginger biscuits on the middle shelf of the preheated oven for 15–17 minutes until golden brown and firm.

Cool on the baking trays.

CHOCOLATE MOUSSE MELTING MOMENTS

I first made these by chance: I was going to use buttercream as a filling but when I opened the fridge I noticed some little pots of mousse I'd made the night before, so I tried them instead. And my, do they work well: they are like the best Bourbons you've tasted. You will need to make the chocolate mousse well in advance.

Melting moments
250g unsalted butter, softened
60g icing sugar
1 tsp vanilla extract
250g plain flour
50g cornflour
60g cocoa powder

Chocolate mousse filling
100g dark chocolate
50g milk chocolate
100ml double cream
1 large egg yolk, beaten
30g icing sugar

You will also need a large baking tray covered in baking parchment and a piping bag fitted with a large open star nozzle

Start by making the chocolate mousse filling. Finely chop the dark and milk chocolate and tip into a bowl. Heat the cream in a small saucepan until it is just below boiling point and then pour over the chopped chocolate and stir gently until the chocolate has melted. Add the egg yolk and icing sugar and stir until smooth and glossy. Chill until set.

Make the melting moments. Combine the butter, icing sugar and vanilla in the bowl of a free-standing mixer or food processor and blend until light and fluffy. Sift the flour, cornflour and cocoa into the bowl and beat until smooth.

Spoon the mixture into a piping bag fitted with a large, open star nozzle and pipe 30 swirls onto the lined baking tray. Chill the melting moments in the fridge for 15 minutes.

Preheat the oven to 180°C/350°F/Gas Mark 4.

Bake the melting moments on the middle shelf of the preheated oven for 12–15 minutes until firm. Leave to cool on the baking tray.

Spoon the chocolate mousse into the clean piping bag; pipe onto 15 of the cookies and then sandwich with the remaining cookies.

Remember – this recipe contains raw egg, so be careful who you feed it to!

VIENNESE FINGERS

These are my middle son Jesse's favourite biscuit. They crumble in the hand and melt in the mouth but they require a light touch and real unsalted butter – margarine simply will not work.

100g unsalted butter, softened
25g icing sugar
1 tsp vanilla extract
100g plain flour
1 tsp cornflour
¼ tsp baking powder
100g milk chocolate, chopped

You will also need a baking tray lined with baking parchment and a piping bag fitted with a medium star nozzle

Preheat the oven to 170°C/325°F/Gas Mark 3.

Tip the butter and sugar into the bowl of a free-standing mixer and beat until pale and light. Add the vanilla extract and mix again. Sift the flour, cornflour and baking powder into the bowl and mix until smooth and thoroughly combined.

Spoon the dough into a piping bag fitted with a medium star nozzle and pipe 10cm-long fingers onto the prepared baking tray. Bake on the middle shelf of the preheated oven for 10–15 minutes until pale golden.

Remove from the oven and cool on the baking trays for 5 minutes. Transfer the cookies to a wire rack until completely cold.

Tip the milk chocolate into a heatproof bowl and melt either in the microwave on a low setting or over a pan of barely simmering water. Remove from the heat and stir until smooth. Dip both ends of the Viennese fingers into the chocolate and leave to set on baking parchment.

COCONUT, RASPBERRY AND WHITE CHOCOLATE KISSES

These flavour combinations work extremely well, and the colours are so pretty it's the sort of thing I'd do at a girly afternoon tea. The freeze-dried raspberries give not only an amazing flavour but also a wonderful texture that almost dances around on your tongue.

175g unsalted butter, softened
110g caster sugar
1 large egg yolk
175g plain flour
25g desiccated coconut
75g ground almonds
100g white chocolate, chopped
20g freeze-dried raspberries

You will also need 2 baking trays lined with baking parchment

Cream the butter and sugar until pale and fluffy in a free-standing mixer or an electric hand whisk or by hand in a bowl with a wooden spoon. Add the egg yolk and beat until combined. Mix in the flour, coconut and ground almonds and beat until the dough comes together into a ball. Wrap in cling film and chill for 30 minutes.

Using your hands roll the dough into 24 even-sized balls – they should be roughly the size of a cherry tomato – and arrange on lined baking trays. Flatten slightly and chill for a further 15 minutes.

Meanwhile, preheat the oven to 170°C/325°F/ Gas Mark 3.

Bake the kisses on the middle shelf of the oven about for 25 minutes until pale golden brown. Cool the cookies on wire racks before filling.

Melt the white chocolate in a heatproof bowl. Stir until smooth and leave to cool and thicken slightly. Meanwhile, crush the freeze-dried raspberries using a pestle and mortar. Add the raspberries to the melted white chocolate.

Spread the flat side of 12 of the cookies with the chocolate and raspberry filling and sandwich with the remaining cookies. Leave to set before serving.

FLORENTINES

For me, these are synonymous with Christmas; they look so effective wrapped in a little clear gift bags, tied with pretty ribbons.

50g unsalted butter
50g soft light brown sugar
50g golden syrup
50g plain flour
20g pecans, roughly chopped
50g flaked almonds
50g dried apricots, chopped
50g dried cranberries
20g desiccated coconut
75g dark chocolate, chopped
75g milk chocolate, chopped

You will also need 2 baking trays lined with baking parchment

Preheat the oven to 180°C/350°F/Gas Mark 4.

Tip the butter, sugar and golden syrup into a medium-sized saucepan and, stirring constantly, melt over a low heat until the sugar has dissolved. Remove from the heat, add the flour, nuts, dried fruit and coconut, and stir well to make sure that everything is coated and thoroughly combined.

Spoon teaspoons of the mixture into little mounds on the lined baking trays, making sure that you leave plenty of space for them to spread during cooking. Bake the florentines in batches on the middle shelf of the preheated oven for 8–10 minutes until golden brown.

Leave the florentines to harden on the baking trays for 30 seconds and then transfer to wire racks to cool completely.

Melt the dark and milk chocolate together in a heatproof bowl, either in the microwave on a low setting or over a pan of barely simmering water. Stir until smooth and leave to cool slightly. Coat the underside of each florentine with a thin layer of chocolate and leave them to set, chocolate-side up, on the cooling racks.

CUSTARD CREAMS

*The boys loved custard creams and what they used to call 'borgones'.
That suited me because I never liked the shop-bought variety of either.*

100g unsalted butter, softened
50g caster sugar
100g plain flour, plus
    extra for rolling out
25g custard powder
25g cornflour

Custard-cream filling
150g icing sugar
45g unsalted butter, softened
20g custard powder
3 tsp full-fat milk

**You will also need a baking tray
lined with baking parchment,
a 6cm square or round cookie
cutter and a piping bag fitted
with a 1cm round nozzle**

To make the biscuits, beat the butter and sugar together until light and fluffy: this can be done either with an electric hand whisk or in a bowl with a wooden spoon. Sift the flour, custard powder and cornflour into the bowl and mix until thoroughly combined and smooth.

Wrap the dough in cling film and chill in the fridge for 20 minutes. Meanwhile, preheat the oven to 170°C/325°F/Gas Mark 3.

Dust the work surface with flour and roll the dough out to a thickness of 3–4mm. Using the cutter, stamp out biscuits and place them on the lined baking tray. Gather any dough off cuts into a ball, then re-roll and stamp out more biscuits.

Pop the baking tray into the fridge to chill for 10 minutes.

Bake on the middle shelf of the preheated oven for 10-12 minutes until the biscuits are pale golden and firm. Leave to cool on the baking tray for a couple of minutes then transfer the biscuits to a wire rack until cold.

To make the filling, mix all the ingredients together until smooth using a hand-held whisk or in the bowl of a free-standing mixer. Spoon into a piping bag fitted with a 1cm round nozzle and pipe the filling onto one half of the biscuits, then sandwich together with the remaining biscuits.

Chapter nine

PASTRY

For a really great pastry, you need to start with great ingredients. The butter must be real butter and very chilled, even after it's come out of the fridge. That's why I keep cold water by me and try not to handle the butter any more than absolutely necessary. The other essential for most short and sweetcrust bakes is blind baking. You need to cover your mixture with parchment paper and fill with baking beans: this keeps the pastry from rising up in the centre as it bakes.

♥

SHORTCRUST

I really like a very short pastry: it can be fiddly to work with but for me it is the best; nothing else bears comparison. I never use margarine as it makes a dreadful, soft unworkable pastry. I find my best pastry is always when I've handled it the least, so I make it in my food processor. This recipe will give you enough pastry for a family pie, top and bottom crust.

250g plain flour, plus extra for rolling out
125g unsalted butter, chilled and diced
a pinch of salt
1 large egg yolk
2–3 tbsp water, chilled

Put the flour, butter and salt into the bowl of a food processor with a metal blade.

Whizz using the pulse button until you have a breadcrumb consistency.

Add the egg yolk, whizz briefly, then add the water a tablespoon at a time until the dough comes together.

Turn onto a floured surface and work very briefly with your hands until smooth. Wrap in cling film and chill for at least half an hour before using.

SWEETCRUST PASTRY

This lovely short pastry is perfect for all kinds of sweet tarts and pies, and with the use of a food processor it is so simple to make.

250g plain flour, plus extra for rolling out
125g unsalted butter, chilled and diced
25g icing or caster sugar
a pinch of salt
2 large egg yolks
2–3 tbsp milk

Put the flour, butter, sugar and salt into the bowl of a food processor with a metal blade.

Whizz with the pulse button until you have a breadcrumb consistency.

Add the egg yolk, whizz briefly, then add the milk one tablespoon at a time until the dough comes together.

Turn onto a lightly floured surface and work very briefly with your hands until the dough is smooth. Wrap in cling film and chill for at least half an hour before using.

ROUGH PUFF PASTRY

The thing with rough puff is just to remember that you need time, as it will require three turns. Also, you should use almost equal amounts of fat and flour. For me, this can be a mixture of butter and white fat, or just butter.

300g plain flour, plus extra for rolling out
a pinch of salt
250g unsalted butter, very chilled or
125g unsalted butter and 125g lard, very chilled
ice cold water

Tip the flour and salt into a large mixing bowl. Coarsely grate the butter (or butter and lard) into the flour, holding the butter in its packet and pulling it down as you go. Using a palette or round edged knife, flick the flour over the grated butter until all of the pieces are covered. Add enough ice cold water to bring the dough together using the knife.

Turn the dough out onto a floured surface and bring together briefly using your hands. Flatten into a rectangle, wrap in cling film and chill for 30 minutes.

On a lightly floured surface, roll the dough out into a rectangle roughly 50 x 15cm. With one of the shorter sides of the rectangle nearest to you, fold the top third down into the middle and the bottom third up over this. You should now have a square measuring one-third of the original size but 3 times as thick. Make a small mark in the dough to indicate which side is the top of the dough square. Wrap in clingflim and chill for at least 30 minutes.

Unwrap the pastry and place the square on the work surface in the same position as it was before, with the mark at the top. Turn the square 90 degrees clockwise and roll out into a neat rectangle roughly 50 x 15cm. Fold the top third down into the middle and the bottom third up over it as before. Make a mark to indicate the top of the square and chill for another 30 minutes.

Repeat this process 2 more times, always making sure that the dough is turned 90 degrees before you start rolling, and chilling the dough in between turns.

ANTIPASTI AND GOATS' CHEESE TART

This is a great tart to serve for lunch. The pastry could be made and chilled the evening before and then it's just a matter of assembling it the next day. I'd say it would serve between four and six people but could be doubled or more to feed bigger parties of people. It's perfect with a rocket salad and a glass of chilled white wine.

1 quantity of rough puff pastry (a 375g pack of fresh supermarket pastry works just as well)
plain flour for rolling out
1 large egg yolk, beaten with 1 tbsp water
150g rindless goats' cheese log
1 packet of vegetable antipasti from the chiller cabinet in the supermarket (150g)
1 tsp fresh thyme, chopped
12 basil leaves
black pepper, freshly ground

You will also need a baking tray covered with baking parchment

Preheat the oven to 210°C/410°F/Gas Mark 6.

Lightly dust the work surface with plain flour and roll out the pastry to a 30 x 10cm rectangle, then place onto the prepared baking tray.

Using the point of a small knife, gently score a border 1cm in from the edge of the rectangle, taking care not to cut all the way through the pastry. Brush the pastry border with the egg wash.

Thinly slice the goats' cheese and lay in 2 lines along the centre of the pastry.

Drain the antipasti of excess oil and arrange the vegetables over the goats' cheese. Sprinkle with thyme and season with freshly ground black pepper.

Bake on the middle shelf of the preheated oven for 25–35 minutes until the pastry is golden brown. Leave to cool for 10 minutes before scattering with basil leaves to serve.

QUICHE LORRAINE

*That's its official name but I call it quiche Jay after my brother,
who ate loads of it to recover his strength after he'd been unwell.*

1 quantity of shortcrust
   pastry (see page 200)
plain flour for rolling out

Filling
1 tbsp olive oil
2 shallots, finely chopped
240g good-quality bacon, diced
400ml double cream
4 large eggs
a splash of lemon juice
50g cheddar cheese, grated
black pepper, freshly ground

You will also need a 20cm tart
tin or flan dish and baking beans

Preheat oven to 180°C/350°F/Gas Mark 4.

Line the flan dish with pastry, pick the base
with a fork, cover with parchment and baking
beans, then chill for half an hour and blind
bake for 15 minutes.

Lightly dust the work surface with flour and
roll the pastry out to a neat disc with a thickness
of about 2mm. Carefully line the tart tin, being
sure to push the pastry neatly into the corners
and trimming off the excess pastry from the top.
Prick the base of the tart shell several times with
a fork. Screw up a sheet of baking parchment
and use to line the inside of the pastry case.
Chill for 10 minutes in the freezer.

Tip the baking beans into the pastry case and
blind bake on a baking tray on the middle shelf
of the oven for 20–25 minutes until pale golden.

Heat the olive oil in a frying pan, add the shallots
and diced bacon and cook slowly until the shallots
are translucent and the bacon starts to brown.

Mix the cream with the eggs, lemon juice and
grated cheese, and season with freshly ground
black pepper.

Tip half of the onion and bacon into the pastry
case and pour over the cream mix – this is best
done on a baking tray in the oven. Sprinkle the
rest of the bacon over the top and bake for
35 minutes until golden and set.

Cool to room temperature to serve.

HONEY AND MUSTARD SAUSAGE ROLLS

When Dylan was younger every Sunday he used to go to rugby. Some weeks they had tournaments where we would spend the day, and sausage rolls with honey and mustard were the team's favourite treat.

plain flour for rolling out
1 quantity of rough puff
 pastry (see page 201)
1 tbsp runny honey
1 tbsp dijon mustard
300g good-quality
 sausages, skinned
1 egg, beaten with
 1 tbsp water
1 tbsp full-fat milk
2 tbsp sesame seeds

Preheat the oven to 180°C/350°F/Gas Mark 4.

Lightly dust the work surface with plain flour and roll the pastry into 2 rectangles each 30 x 15cm.

Mix the honey and mustard together and brush a line down the centre of each pastry rectangle. Using your hands, shape the meat into two long sausages, each the same length as the pastry rectangles, and place one on each piece of pastry on top of the honey and mustard.

Mix the egg yolk with the milk and brush along the long side of each of the pastry rectangles.

Roll the pastry around the sausage meat to completely encase with the seam underneath. Brush the top of the sausage roll with egg wash, sprinkle with sesame seeds and slice into 3–5cm pieces.

Place the sausage rolls on baking trays seam-side down and bake in the preheated oven for 25–30 minutes until golden brown.

CREAM SLICE

*This isn't like anything you would ever have bought in a baker's.
It is light as air and vibrant in colour – everything that a
British summer dessert should be.*

1 quantity rough puff pastry
(see page 201)
icing sugar to finish
plain flour for rolling out
400ml double cream
100ml good-quality,
ready-made custard
400g strawberries
3 tbsp strawberry jam
6 whole, small strawberries
to garnish

**You will also need 3 baking
trays covered with baking
parchment and a piping bag
fitted with a large star nozzle**

Preheat the oven to 220°C/425°F/Gas Mark 7.

Cut the pastry into 3 equal-sized pieces and roll
each piece out on a lightly floured work surface
into a 30 x 15cm rectangle. Place the pastry on
the prepared baking trays, prick all over with
a fork and chill for 30 minutes.

Bake the pastry in the preheated oven for about
12 minutes until golden.

Dust with icing sugar and bake for another
5–7 minutes until golden and caramelized.
Leave the pastry tiles on wire racks until cold.

Whip the double cream until it will hold a peak,
fold in the custard and spoon into a piping bag.
Hull and slice the strawberries.

To assemble, place the most unattractive pastry
tile on your serving plate. Pipe vertical lines of the
cream over the pastry to cover completely. Drop
little half teaspoons of jam randomly onto the
cream and top with half of the sliced strawberries.

Spread a little cream on the underside of the
second pastry tile and place over the strawberries.
Repeat the whole process for the second layer.

Dust with icing sugar and finish with 3 whole
strawberries on each end.

APPLE AND RASPBERRY MERINGUE PIE

The original recipe for this came from my Auntie Helen. When I was researching for the Bake Off, she remembered an apple one that she used to bake and I came up with the idea of adding raspberries.

plain flour for
   rolling out
1 quantity sweetcrust
   pastry (see page 200)
1 egg, beaten with
   1 tbsp water
900g Bramley
   cooking apples,
   peeled and sliced
30g unsalted butter
185g caster sugar
zest of 2 lemons,
   finely grated
2 tsp cornflour
3 eggs, separated
400g raspberries

**You will also need
a 23cm tart tin with
a depth of about 3½cm
and baking beans**

Preheat your oven to 190°C/375°F/Gas Mark 5.

Dust the work surface with flour and roll the pastry out into a neat disc with a thickness of about 2mm. Line the tart tin, being sure to push the pastry neatly into the corners and trimming off the excess. Prick the base of the tart shell several times with a fork. Screw up a sheet of baking parchment and use to line the inside of the pastry case. Chill for 10 minutes in the freezer.

Tip baking beans into the pastry case and blind bake on the middle shelf of the oven for 20–25 minutes until pale golden. Remove the baking parchment and beans, brush the pastry case with egg wash and reduce the oven temperature to 170°C/325°F/Gas Mark 3. Bake for a further 5 minutes.

Peel, core and dice the apples, tip into a saucepan and add the butter, 60g of caster sugar, the lemon zest and 100ml of water. Cook until the apples have reduced to a dry purée. Stir frequently to prevent them sticking and burning on the bottom of the pan. Remove from the heat and cool slightly. Mix the cornflour with 2 teaspoons of cold water and add to the apple purée along with the egg yolks. Beat until smooth and combined.

Spoon the apples into the baked sweetcrust pastry case, spread level and arrange the raspberries evenly in the apple purée.

In a clean, dry bowl whisk the egg whites until stiff. Gradually add the remaining 125g caster sugar, whisking well between each addition, until the meringue is stiff and glossy.

Spoon the meringue on top of the apples and bake for 15 minutes until very lightly golden. Leave the tart to cool and then chill in the fridge before serving.

TREACLE TART

This reminds me of Langan's Restaurant, where we would sometimes go for special girly birthdays, and of one friend in particular who would always have the treacle tart. So, Candy, this one is for you.

1 quantity of shortcrust
   pastry (see page 200) you
   could use sweetcrust but
   I find the short a much
   better balance of sweetness
plain flour for rolling out
400g golden syrup
5 large eggs
finely grated zest and
   juice of 2 lemons
150g fresh breadcrumbs

**You will also need a
20 x 30cm loose bottomed
flan tin and baking beans**

Lightly dust the work surface with flour and roll the pastry out into a neat rectangle with a thickness of about 2mm. Carefully line the tart tin, being sure to push the pastry neatly into the corners and trimming off the excess from the top. Prick the base of the tart shell several times with a fork. Screw up a sheet of baking parchment and use to line the inside of the pastry case. Chill for 10 minutes in the freezer.

Preheat the oven to 190°C/375°F./Gas Mark 5.

Tip baking beans into the pastry case and blind bake on the middle shelf of the preheated oven for 20–25 minutes until pale golden. Remove the baking parchment and beans, reduce the oven temperature to 170°C/325°F/Gas Mark 3 and bake the pastry case for a further 5 minutes.

In a large bowl, mix together the syrup (I find it easier to weigh the syrup straight into the bowl), eggs, lemon zest and juice. Add the breadcrumbs and mix until thoroughly combined.

Pour into the pastry case and bake in a oven for 30–35 minutes until golden.

Leave the tart to set for 10 minutes in the tin before cutting into slices to serve.

BABY PECAN PIES

All my friends have a favourite bake that I do and this is the favourite of my beautiful Tracy. We have been friends for as long as I remember, and she is gorgeous both inside and out.

plain flour for rolling out
½ quantity of sweetcrust
    pastry (see page 200)
200ml maple syrup, plus
    a little extra to glaze
50g unsalted butter
40g light soft brown sugar
60g caster sugar
120g pecans, chopped
2 large eggs, whisked
    in a small jug
1 tsp vanilla extract
2 tbsp flour

You will also need a 9cm
round cutter, a 12-hole
muffin tin and baking beans

Preheat the oven to 180°C/350°F/Gas Mark 4.

Roll out the pastry on a lightly floured surface to a thickness of no more than 2mm. Use the cutter to stamp out 12 pastry circles. Place the circles into the muffin tin, making sure to push the pastry well into the corners. Line each hole with a piece of baking parchment and fill with baking beans. Chill for 30 minutes.

Blind bake the pastry cases on the middle shelf of the preheated oven for 10 minutes, then remove the paper and beans and bake for a further 5 minutes until lightly golden.

Tip the maple syrup, butter, soft light brown and caster sugar into a saucepan and melt over a low heat until combined. Remove from the heat, add the pecans, eggs, vanilla and flour, and mix until smooth.

Pour into pastry cases and bake for 15 minutes until set. Leave the mini pies to rest for 10 minutes in the muffin tin and then carefully ease out and leave to cool on wire racks. Brush with a little extra warmed maple syrup to finish.

BAKEWELL TART

Sometimes when I want something really comforting I make myself a Bakewell – it's so homely and it just has that restorative property that only a good bake can provide. Serve with a cup of tea or as a dessert with custard: it's fab either way.

plain flour for rolling out
1 quantity of sweet crust
   pastry (see page 200)
150g self-raising flour
150g unsalted butter, softened
150g caster sugar
50g ground almonds
3 large eggs
1 tsp almond extract
5 tbsp strawberry jam
50g flaked almonds
icing sugar for dusting

You will also need a 23cm tart tin with a depth of about 3.5cm and baking beans

Lightly dust the work surface with flour and roll the pastry out into a neat disc with a thickness of about 2mm. Carefully line the tart tin, being sure to push the pastry neatly into the corners and trimming off the excess from the top. Prick the base of the tart shell several times with a fork. Screw up a sheet of baking parchment and use to line the inside of the pastry case. Chill for 10 minutes in the freezer.

Preheat the oven to 190°C/375°F/Gas Mark 5.

Tip baking beans into the pastry case and blind bake on the middle shelf of the preheated oven for 20–25 minutes until pale golden. Remove the baking parchment and beans. Reduce the oven temperature to 170°C/325°F/Gas Mark 3 and bake the pastry case for a further 5 minutes.

To make the filling, tip the flour, butter, sugar, ground almonds and eggs into the bowl of the food processor and blend until smooth. Add the almond extract.

Spread the strawberry jam over the base of the tart shell and carefully spoon the batter on top in an even layer. Scatter with flaked almonds and bake on the middle shelf of the oven for 40 minutes until golden. If the top of the tart starts to brown too quickly, loosely cover the tart with a sheet of foil.

Leave the tart to cool to room temperature before dusting with icing sugar to serve.

PLUM FRANGIPANE

I think plums are underrated: they have the most wonderful flavour and work so well in a frangipane.

plain flour for rolling out
1 quantity of sweetcrust
    pastry (see page 200)
50g hazelnuts, chopped
175g unsalted butter, softened
175g caster sugar
3 large eggs and 1 yolk
150g self-raising flour
100g ground almonds
½ tsp cinnamon
6 plums, firm

You will also need a 23cm
tart tin with a depth of about
3.5cm and baking beans

Lightly dust the work surface with flour and roll the pastry out into a neat disc with a thickness of about 2mm. Carefully line the tart tin, being sure to push the pastry neatly into the corners and trimming off the excess pastry from the top. Prick the base of the tart shell several times with a fork. Screw up a sheet of baking parchment and use to line the inside of the pastry case. Chill for 10 minutes in the freezer.

Preheat the oven to 180°C/350°F/Gas Mark 4.

Tip baking beans into the pastry case and blind bake on the middle shelf of the preheated oven for 20–25 minutes until pale golden. Remove the baking parchment and beans. Reduce the oven temperature to 170°C/325°F/Gas Mark 3 and bake the pastry case for a further 5 minutes.

Tip the hazelnuts onto a baking tray and lightly toast in the hot oven. Cool slightly and finely chop.

To make the filling mix together the butter, sugar, eggs, egg yolk, flour, ground almonds and cinnamon until light and fluffy. Fold in the chopped toasted hazelnuts. Spoon the frangipane into the pastry case and spread level. Cut the plums into quarters and arrange evenly spaced, skin side up around the tart. Bake for 35-45 minutes or until golden, if the tart starts to colour too quickly, cover loosely with foil.

Leave to cool in the tin for 10 minutes then transfer to a wire rack to cool completely.

ONION AND PORT SALUT TART

The slowly cooked onions and the creamy Port Salut work so well together, all that is needed is a few salad leaves for the perfect lunch.

10g unsalted butter
2 tbsp olive oil
750g onions, sliced
2 tsp soft light brown sugar
plain flour for rolling out
1 quantity of shortcrust
    pastry (see page 200)
250ml double cream
100ml full-fat milk
4 large eggs
a pinch of salt
thyme
185g Port Salut cheese

You will also need a 23cm
tart tin with a depth of about
3.5cm and baking beans

Preheat the oven to 180°C/350°F/Gas Mark 4.

Melt the butter and olive oil in a large pan, add the onions and set the pan over a low heat. Cook the onions slowly for about 30 minutes until very soft. Once the onions have sweated down, add the brown sugar and cook for a further 5 minutes, remove from the heat and leave to cool.

Lightly dust the work surface with flour and roll the pastry out into a neat disc with a thickness of about 2mm. Carefully line the tart tin, being sure to push the pastry neatly into the corners and trimming off the excess from the top. Prick the base of the tart shell several times with a fork. Screw up a sheet of baking parchment and use to line the inside of the pastry case. Chill for 10 minutes in the freezer.

Tip baking beans into the pastry case and blind bake on the middle shelf of the oven for 20–25 minutes. Remove the baking parchment and beans. Reduce the oven temperature to 170°C/325°F/Gas Mark 3 and bake for a further 5 minutes.

Remove the pastry case and increase the oven temperature to 180°C/350°F/Gas Mark 4.

Mix together the cream, milk, eggs, salt and thyme. Spoon the onions into the tin and pour over the cream mixture. Break the cheese into small chunks and pop evenly into the tart. Cook the tart on a baking tray for 35 minutes or until golden and slightly wobbly in the centre.

Leave to set in the tin before turning out and cutting.

TOFFEE APPLE CRUMBLY PIE

This pie is just one sheet of pastry, with the edges folded over the filling.
If any pieces break off you can just crumble them over the top!

315g dessert apples
plain flour for rolling out
1 quantity of sweetcrust
    pastry (see page 200)
1 egg white, beaten
45g soft dark brown sugar
45g unsalted butter, softened
2 tbsp caster sugar

You will also need
a large baking tray

Preheat the oven to 200°C/400°F/Gas Mark 6.

Place the baking tray in the oven to heat up while you prepare the pie.

Peel, core and dice the apples.

Lightly dust the work surface with flour and roll out the pastry to a circle roughly 30cm in diameter and slide onto piece of baking parchment. Brush the pastry with egg white and place the diced apples in the middle, leaving a pastry border of about 5–7cm all around. Sprinkle the brown sugar evenly over the apples and dot with the butter.

Fold the pastry border up and over the apples, brush with egg white and sprinkle with half of the caster sugar. Slide the pie onto the hot baking tray and cook on the middle shelf of the oven for about 15 minutes until starting to brown. Sprinkle with the remaining sugar and bake for a further 10-15 minutes until the apples are tender and the pastry is crisp.

Serve with fresh cream or custard.

STEAK AND MUSHROOM PIE

I think this steak pie is so luxurious that the only accompaniments it needs are some fresh garden peas and creamy horseradish mash.

6 tbsp olive oil

20g unsalted butter

300g button mushrooms, wiped clean

200g red onion, sliced

3 tbsp plain flour, plus extra for rolling out

a pinch of salt

black pepper, freshly ground

1.5 kg of braising steak, diced

40g dried mixed mushrooms

3 Oxo cubes

1 glass of red wine

1 bouquet garni

1 quantity of rough puff pastry (see page 201)

1 egg, beaten with 1 tbsp water

You will also need a large pie dish

In your largest pan, heat the oil with the butter. Add the button mushrooms and sliced red onions and cook until softened. Remove from the pan and set aside on a plate.

Tip the plain flour onto a large plate and season with salt and pepper. Toss the diced beef in the seasoned flour and brown in the hot pan in batches. Add more butter or oil to the pan as needed. As the meat browns, remove it from the pan and add to the plate with the button mushrooms and onions.

While you are browning the beef, cover the dried mushrooms with 500ml of boiling water and leave for about 5-10 minutes to soften in a bowl.

Return the beef, onions and mushrooms to the pan. Add the dried mushrooms and their soaking liquid plus another 500ml of water, the Oxo cubes, the red wine and the bouquet garni and stir well. Bring to the boil, cover and place in the oven at 120°C/250°F/Gas Mark ½ for about 4 hours, checking and adding more water if the liquid is getting too low.

Once the meat is really tender, remove from the heat, check the seasoning and add a knob of butter for a lovely shine. Transfer into a large pie dish and leave to cool slightly.

On a floured work surface, roll the pastry out so that it is slightly larger than the top of your pie dish. Brush the edges of the dish with egg wash and lay the pastry on top, trim the edges and brush with egg wash.

Turn the oven up to 190°C/375°F/Gas Mark 5 and bake the pie for about 30 minutes until bubbling and the pastry is golden brown, serve immediately.

Chapter
ten

DESSERTS

*For me, sometimes the pudding is better than the
main event. I adore home-made puddings and feel
so let down when I've been to restaurants where
only those dreadful prepackaged desserts are on
offer. Especially when I know how easy it can
be to make something great from scratch.*

♥

PASSION FRUIT SWISS ROLL

This is a lovely light dessert, perfect for a summer barbecue. You can make it in the morning and keep it covered in the fridge until you're ready to serve.

4 large eggs
100g caster sugar
80g self-raising flour
25g cornflour
4 tbsp caster sugar
    for sprinkling

Filling
3 passion fruits
150ml double cream
100ml Greek yogurt
25g icing sugar, plus
    extra for dusting
zest of half an orange,
    finely grated

You will also need a 33 x 23cm Swiss roll tin lined with a sheet of buttered baking parchment

Preheat the oven to 180°C/350°F/Gas Mark 4.

Whisk the eggs and 100g caster sugar together until doubled in volume, light and fluffy.

Sieve the flour and cornflour together, and using a metal spoon, fold into the egg and sugar mixture one third at a time. Spoon into the prepared tin and spread level.

Bake on the middle shelf of the preheated oven for 10 minutes until golden and springy to the touch.

Meanwhile, lay a large sheet of baking parchment on a work surface and sprinkle with 4 tablespoons of caster sugar. Remove the Swiss roll from the oven and turn it out onto the sugared parchment. Peel off the original buttered baking paper. Trim the edges of the cake and then roll up, starting at one of the shorter ends and with the sugared parchment inside the roll. Cover with a slightly damp tea towel and leave until cold.

To make the filling, cut the passion fruit in half and scoop the seeds and juice into a bowl.

In another bowl, whip the cream, Greek yogurt, icing sugar and orange zest until the mixture will hold soft peaks. Lightly fold the passion fruit into the cream to create a marbled effect.

Carefully unroll the sponge and spread evenly with the passion fruit cream. Re-roll the cake using the sugared paper to help support it as you do so.

Place on a serving dish and lightly dust with icing sugar to serve.

RHUBARB CRÈME BRÛLÉE

Rhubarb crème brûlée is a part of the best dessert I've ever eaten, a trio called 'rhubarb, rhubarb, rhubarb' that is one of the specialities of a really posh restaurant in London. This isn't the same recipe but it tastes really good.

450g rhubarb
1 piece of stem ginger,
**   finely chopped**
juice of half an orange
2 tbsp soft brown sugar
4 large egg yolks
1 tsp vanilla extract
4–6 tbsp caster sugar
300ml full-fat milk
300ml double cream

You will also need
4 ramekins

Preheat the oven to 170°C/325°F/Gas Mark 3.

Chop the rhubarb into 1cm pieces and put into a baking dish with the ginger, pour over the orange juice and sprinkle with sugar. Bake in a preheated oven for 30 minutes, then remove and turn down the oven to 120°C/250°F/Gas Mark ½.

Spoon the strained rhubarb into 4 ramekin dishes.

Whisk the egg yolks, vanilla extract and sugar until light and fluffy.

Heat the milk and cream in a saucepan until just below boiling.

Add to the egg yolks and sugar, whisk vigorously, strain and pour equal amounts into the ramekin dishes.

Put ramekins into a baking tray and half fill with boiling water.

Bake in the oven for 40 minutes.

Leave until cool, then chill completely in the fridge.

Top each brûlée with a tablespoon of caster sugar and melt it using a blowtorch.

BAKED CHEESECAKE

This sort of cheesecake is my favourite: it reminds me of New York.
It's creamy and light and an absolute dream to make.

70g unsalted butter, melted
10 digestive biscuits
600g full-fat cream cheese
2 tbsp plain flour
175g caster sugar
2 tsp vanilla extract
2 large eggs
1 large egg yolk
284ml sour cream
2 tbsp icing sugar, sifted

Topping
De-stalk, hull and slice
5 strawberries per person,
place in a bowl and sprinkle
with caster sugar. Peel half
an orange per person and
slice the segments between
the membranes allowing to
drop into the bowl. Mix well
and serve at room temperature
on top of the chesecake.

You will also need a
20cm springform cake
tin, lightly greased

Preheat the oven to 180°C/350°F/Gas Mark 4.

Melt the butter in a small pan or in the microwave.

Crush the biscuits in a food processor and tip into a
bowl. Add the melted butter and mix to thoroughly
combine. Press the buttery crumbs into the base
of the springform tin in an even layer.

Bake on the middle shelf of the preheated oven for
5 minutes. Remove from the oven and cool while
you prepare the filing.

Beat the cream cheese until smooth, then add the flour,
sugar, vanilla extract, eggs, yolk, and half of the sour
cream and beat again until smooth, light and fluffy.
Carefully pour into the tin and spread until level.

Place on a baking tray and bake on the middle shelf of
the preheated oven for 30 minutes until only just set.
Remove from the oven and leave to rest for 5 minutes.

Mix the remaining sour cream with the icing sugar
and very carefully spoon over the top of the cheesecake
in an even layer.

Return to the oven for a further 10 minutes until
just set but still very slightly wobbly in the centre.

Leave the cheesecake to cool in the tin and then
chill in the fridge for at least 4 hours or overnight
until ready to serve.

ORANGE LIQUEUR BREAD AND BUTTER PUDDING

If you want an adult nursery food this is your dish: the lovely soft pudding centre with the crispy corners burnished with orange jam, Cointreau- or Grand Marnier-soaked sultanas, and creamy custard.

200g sultanas
30ml orange liqueur
100g caster sugar
zest of 1 large or 2 small oranges
½ tsp nutmeg, freshly grated
1 medium loaf of white bread
100g unsalted butter, softened
3 large eggs
4 large yolks
300ml double cream
200ml full-fat milk
4 tbsp orange and ginger jam

Soak the sultanas in the orange liqueur for 2 hours before you start to prepare the pudding so that they plump up and become juicy.

Mix the sugar, orange zest and nutmeg in a small bowl.

Remove the crusts from the bread and cut into 2cm-thick slices. Generously spread the slices with the soft butter.

Lay a slice of buttered bread in a heatproof dish and scatter with sugar mix and sultanas. Repeat layering until the dish is full and you have used up all of the ingredients.

Whisk together the eggs, egg yolks, cream and milk. Strain and slowly pour over the bread. Cover with foil and leave for at least 1 hour in the fridge.

Preheat the oven to 180°C/350°F/Gas Mark 4.

Bake on the middle shelf of the preheated oven, covered with foil, for 30 minutes until golden brown.

Warm the jam and pass through a sieve to remove any lumps. Brush the top of the pudding with the jam and return to the oven for another 15 minutes or until golden, caramelized and crispy on the corners.

Leave to stand for 10 minutes before serving.

RHUBARB CRUMBLE

Crumble reminds me of real nursery food, home cooking, comfort food at its best. I love to add new flavours to old favourites and, with the vanilla sugar to bring out the taste of the rhubarb and the little amaretti biscuits to give yet more flavour and also a wonderful texture, I think this is a wonderful pudding, perfect for a Sunday lunch to share with the family.

500g rhubarb
50g vanilla sugar
   (see pages 248–9)
200g plain flour
130g unsalted butter, chilled
   and diced
100g demerara sugar
50g amaretti biscuits

You will also need a 23cm round dish and a baking tray

Preheat the oven to 200°C/400°F/Gas Mark 6.

Trim the rhubarb and cut into 5cm pieces. Place on a baking tray, sprinkle with the vanilla sugar and bake in the preheated oven for about 10 minutes until just tender. Remove from the heat and cool.

To make the crumble, combine the flour, butter, demerara sugar and biscuits in the bowl of a food processor and pulse until you have a crumble texture.

Spoon the rhubarb into a 23cm round dish, sprinkle over the crumble topping and bake for 30–35 minutes until the fruit is bubbling and the crumble is golden.

Leave to stand for 5 minutes before serving with extra-thick double cream or ice cream.

BOOZY ESSEX CHERRY FRANGIPANE TART

This pudding came about one evening when I was out with a group of friends. We were all talking about my book and they asked if I could name a recipe after them. So this is it, another memory in the making.

1 quantity of sweetcrust
   pastry (see page 200)
160g tinned cherries,
   pitted and drained
4–5 tbsp cherry brandy or port
150g self-raising flour
2 egg yolks, 1 beaten with
   3 tbsp water
175g unsalted butter, softened
175g caster sugar
3 large eggs
50g ground almonds
50g desiccated coconut

You will also need a 23cm tart tin with a depth of about 3.5cm, a small heart-shaped cutter and baking beans

Preheat the oven to 190°C/375°F/Gas Mark 5.

The day before you bake this tart you will need to soak the cherries in 4–5 tablespoons of cherry brandy or port. Cover with cling film and set aside.

Dust the work surface with flour and roll the pastry out into a neat disc with a thickness of about 2mm. Line the tart tin and push the pastry into the corners. Prick the base of the tart shell with a fork. Screw up a sheet of baking parchment and use to line the inside of the pastry case. Chill for 10 minutes in the freezer.

Using a small heart or star cutter, stamp out little shapes from the leftover pastry trimmings.

Tip baking beans into the case and blind bake in the middle of the oven for 20–25 minutes until pale golden. Remove the parchment and beans and brush with the egg wash. Reduce the oven temperature to 170°C/325°F/Gas Mark 3 and bake for a further 5 minutes.

To make the frangipane cream the butter, sugar, eggs, yolk, flour, almonds and coconut in the bowl of a free-standing mixer or with a hand-held electric whisk, and beat until smooth, light and fluffy. Strain the cherries and fold into the batter.

Spoon the mixture into the pastry case and spread level. Brush the pastry hearts with egg wash and place over the top of the frangipane. Place on a baking tray and bake for 45 minutes until golden and firm.

Leave the tart to cool in the tin for 15-20 minutes and then transfer to a wire rack until cold.

STRAWBERRY CREAM CHOCOLATE CUPS

My friend Frances has been one of my chief tasters over the years and she deemed these amazing – high praise indeed from the queen of sugar. Dylan, my youngest, thought them fantastic and asked me to make up some more immediately, so I think they may be a winner.

300g milk chocolate, chopped
200g full-fat cream cheese
200ml double cream
100g icing sugar
400g strawberries, hulled,
   plus extra to serve
3 Crunchie bars or 100g
   honeycomb, bashed with
   a rolling pin

You will also need a muffin
tin lined with 6 paper cases
and a large piping bag fitted
with a large star nozzle

Bits & Bobs

Chocolate chip cookies
Sometimes you just fancy
something sweet but don't have
enough time or energy to bake.
I always keep home-made chocolate
chip cookies in the freezer for
such a moment – they defrost fast
and can be made into a delicious
dessert with minimum effort.
See pages 248–9.

Melt half the chocolate in a heatproof bowl in the microwave on a low setting or over a pan of barely simmering water.

Stir until smooth and, using a pastry brush, coat the inside of each paper muffin case with a neat layer of melted chocolate. Pop in the fridge for at least 2 hours or until firm.

Melt the rest of the chocolate in the same way, cool slightly and paint the cups with a second layer of chocolate concentrating on the sides. Chill again until firm.

Whip the cream cheese, double cream and 50g of the icing sugar until the mixture will hold a peak. Whizz the strawberries and remaining icing sugar in a blender and pass through a sieve. Fold half of the strawberry purée into the cream mixture and spoon into a piping bag fitted with a star nozzle.

Very carefully peel the paper cases off the chocolate cups and place a tablespoon of the remaining strawberry purée into the bottom of each. Pipe a tall swirl of the strawberry cream into the chocolate cups, scatter with the honeycomb pieces and a few slices of strawberry to serve.

HAZELNUT AND CHOCOLATE TART

My middle son Jesse really loves Ferrero Rocher — this one's for him.

plain flour for rolling out
1 quantity seetcrust pastry
   (see page 200)
1 large egg yolk, beaten
   with 1 tbsp water
100g blanched hazelnuts
350g milk chocolate,
   chopped really fine
150g dark chocolate
   (72% cocoa solids),
   chopped really fine
400ml double cream
4 tbsp chocolate
   hazelnut spread

**You will also need a 23cm
tart tin with a depth of about
3.5cm and baking beans**

Preheat the oven to 190°C/375°F/Gas Mark 5.

Dust the work surface with flour and roll the pastry out in to a neat disc with a thickness of about 2mm. Carefully line the tart tin, being sure to push the pastry neatly into the corners. Prick the base of the tart shell several times with a fork. Screw up a sheet of baking parchment and use to line the inside of the pastry case. Chill for 10 minutes in the freezer.

Tip baking beans into the pastry case and blind bake on the middle shelf of the preheated oven for 20–25 minutes until pale golden. Remove the baking parchment and beans and lightly brush the inside of the pastry case with the egg wash.

Reduce the oven temperature to 170°C/325°F/ Gas Mark 3 and bake the pastry case for a further 5 minutes.

While the oven is still hot, toast the hazelnuts on a baking tray for about 5 minutes until golden. Remove from the oven, set aside and cool.

Tip the chopped milk and dark chocolate into a saucepan, add the cream and place over a low heat. Stir constantly until smooth and the chocolate has melted. Add the hazelnut spread and stir until thoroughly combined. Pour the chocolate cream into the cooled pastry case and chill for a couple of hours until set.

Roughly chop the toasted hazelnuts and scatter over the top of the tart to serve. Warm a large knife under hot water, dry and cut the tart into neat slices.

INDIVIDUAL BLUEBERRY BRÛLÉE CHEESECAKES

These are so simple: you just give everything a little stir, pop it into the oven, chill in the fridge, then add a sprinkle of sugar and you have the loveliest little dessert. Leave the caramelizing of the sugar until just before serving because if you re-chill for too long, the sugar starts to melt.

55g unsalted butter
6 digestive biscuits
300g full-fat cream cheese
100ml Greek yogurt
100g caster sugar
2 large eggs
1 tsp vanilla extract
100g blueberries

To serve
8 tsp caster sugar

You will also need a muffin tin lined with 8 paper muffin cases and a kitchen blowtorch

Preheat the oven to 180°C/350°F/Gas Mark 4.

Melt 30g of the butter in a small pan or in the microwave. Crush the digestive biscuits in a food processor and tip into a bowl. Add the melted butter and mix to thoroughly combine. Spoon the buttery crumbs into the muffin cases and press into the bases to form a crust. Bake on the middle shelf of the preheated oven for 5 minutes and then leave to cool.

Beat together the cream cheese, Greek yogurt, caster sugar, eggs and vanilla. Melt the remaining butter, add to the mixture and stir until thoroughly combined.

Spoon the mixture evenly between the muffin cases, add the blueberries and bake for 25 minutes in the preheated oven.

Leave the cheesecakes to cool before chilling in the fridge for at least 2 hours.

Just before serving, sprinkle each cheesecake with a teaspoon of caster sugar and caramelize with a blowtorch. Leave for a couple of minutes for the caramel to set and then serve straight away.

ETON MESS

What is not to like about Eton mess? Even the name always makes me smile. I like to think it must come from the mess in the dorms at Eton, which may be taken as evidence that teenagers are untidy wherever they go to college, school or university which is a comfort to a mum of three messy boys.

2 egg whites
1 tsp lemon juice
420g caster sugar
500g strawberries, hulled
600ml double cream
fresh mint leaves, optional

You will also need a piping bag fitted with a 1cm plain nozzle and a baking tray covered with baking parchment

Preheat the oven to 100°C/212°F/Gas Mark 2.

Make the meringues first. Whisk the egg whites with the lemon juice until they will hold soft peaks. Gradually add 120g of caster sugar, mixing well between each addition until the meringue is bright white, stiff and glossy.

Spoon into a piping bag fitted with a 1cm plain nozzle and pipe 2–3cm mounds onto the prepared baking tray.

Bake on the middle shelf of the preheated oven for 1 hour until crisp and dry. Turn the oven off and leave the meringues to cool inside.

With a fork, roughly mash half of the strawberries and tip into a saucepan with the remaining 300g of caster sugar. Slowly bring to the boil, stirring to dissolve the sugar, then turn down the heat to low-medium and continue to cook for 15 minutes until thickened to a soft jam consistency. Pour into a bowl and leave to cool before chilling until ready to use.

Quarter the remaining strawberries. In a large bowl, whip the cream until it holds soft peaks, add the quartered strawberries and the whole mini meringues and fold together using a large metal spoon.

Place a tablespoon of the strawberry jam into the bottom of 6 sundae glasses or tumblers. Lightly fold a few tablespoons of the jam through the cream, then spoon into the sundae glasses and top with a mint leaf.

SPICED-APPLE STEAMED PUDDING

A lovely cosy pudding and a real winter winner in my eyes. The first time I made it, Billy's friend Frank had two helpings and took the rest home.

30g unsalted butter
2 Bramley cooking apples,
   peeled and diced
30g soft brown sugar
1 tsp ground cinnamon

Sponge
150g unsalted butter
150g caster sugar
3 large eggs
150g self-raising flour
3 tbsp full-fat milk

To serve
20g unsalted butter, softened

You will also need a
1.2 litre (2 pint) pudding
basin, buttered

Make the apple topping first. Melt the butter in a frying pan, add the apples and cook over a gentle heat until they start to soften. Add the soft brown sugar and continue to cook until melted, and the apples are juicy but still hold their shape.

Stir in the cinnamon and spoon the apples into the buttered basin, making sure that you get all of the juices.

To make the sponge, tip the butter, sugar, eggs, flour and milk into the food processor and whizz until smooth.

Spoon the sponge mixture into the basin: cover all of the apple mixture. Lay a sheet of baking parchment over the bowl, top with a sheet of foil and pleat the two together in the middle to allow space for the sponge to rise. Fold the paper and foil over the sides and tie securely with kitchen string.

Put the bowl into a steamer, or a large saucepan with a saucer inverted on the bottom, pour boiling water to come halfway up the sides of the bowl and steam for 2 hours.

Run a palette knife around the edge of the sponge to loosen the sides and turn the pudding out of the bowl and onto a warmed serving dish. Melt the remaining 20g of butter in the warm pudding basin and pour over the sponge, along with any apple pieces that remain in the bottom of the bowl.

STICKY TOFFEE PUDDING

*This for me is a perfect autumn dessert: a light, moist, fruity sponge
and a creamy toffee sauce – it's so good. If I'm having a dinner party,
I make the sponge and the sauce in the morning and just gently
reheat under a low grill in individual portions.*

200g dried dates or prunes
70g unsalted butter, softened
175g soft brown sugar
3 tbsp golden syrup
2 large eggs, beaten
200g self-raising flour
1 tsp bicarbonate of soda
250ml water, boiling

Toffee sauce
150g soft dark brown sugar
100g unsalted butter
250ml double cream

**You will also need a 23cm
square baking tin, buttered
and lined with buttered
baking parchment**

Preheat the oven to 200°C/400°F/Gas Mark 6.

Tip the dates or prunes into a bowl and pour over
the boiling water; cover and leave for 10 minutes
to soften.

Cream the butter and sugar in the bowl of a
free-standing mixer until light and fluffy.

Slowly add the golden syrup and beaten eggs
and mix well to combine. Sieve the flour into
the bowl and mix again until smooth.

Add the bicarbonate of soda to the dried fruit
and water mixture and, using a hand-held blender
or food processor, whizz to a purée. Fold into the
batter and spoon into the prepared tin.

Bake on the middle shelf of the oven for about
40 minutes until well risen and a skewer inserted
into the middle of the pudding comes out clean.

Meanwhile, prepare the toffee sauce. Put all of
the ingredients into a saucepan over a medium
heat and stir until everything is melted and well
combined. Bring to the boil and simmer gently
for 30 seconds to 1 minute.

Cut the hot pudding into squares and serve
with the sauce.

LITTLE HOT CHOCOLATE AND LIME PUDDINGS

These are great little fondant-type puddings. The lime zest gives them a real zing and brings the chocolate alive. You can make these up to a day before they're needed, and just keep them in the fridge until you're ready to bake. They're perfect for dinner with friends because you'll be back at the table within seven minutes.

100g good dark
   chocolate, chopped
100g unsalted butter
2 large eggs
100g caster sugar
zest of 1 lime, finely grated
40g self-raising flour
30g cocoa powder
tsp baking powder

You will also need
6 large ramekins

Melt the chocolate and butter in a small bowl either in the microwave on a low setting or over a pan of barely simmering water. Stir until smooth and remove from the heat.

Whisk together the eggs and sugar until really light and fluffy. You should be able to leave ribbons of mixture on the top when you lift the whisk from the bowl.

Fold the melted chocolate, butter and grated lime zest into the mixture. Sift the flour, cocoa and baking powder into the bowl and fold in using a large metal spoon.

Spoon the mixture into 6 ramekin dishes and chill in the fridge for at least 1 hour.

Preheat the oven to 200°C/400°F/Gas Mark 6.

Bake the puddings on a baking tray on the middle shelf of the preheated oven for about 7 minutes; the top should be baked and the middles should be soft.

SUMMER PUDDING

This is a lovely tasting pudding: the addition of the lemon grass syrup gives it a really fresh flavour and the stunning colours of summer make it a centrepiece for any table.

3 sticks of lemon grass
175g caster sugar
200g redcurrants
200g blackcurrants
500g blueberries
500g raspberries
500g blackberries
400g loaf of brioche cut into 1cm thick slices

You will also need a 1.2 litre (2 pint) pudding basin

Bruise the lemongrass by bashing it once or twice with a rolling pin. Put the lemongrass and caster sugar into a saucepan, add 3 tablespoons of water and set the pan over a low heat to dissolve the sugar. Boil for 30 seconds, remove from the heat and leave to cool and infuse for a couple of hours.

Remove the stalks from the redcurrants and blackcurrants and put the fruit into a saucepan along with the blueberries, raspberries and blackberries.

Strain the syrup into the pan and discard the lemongrass. Slowly bring to the boil, turn the heat down low and cook gently until the fruit is tender but still holds its shape.

Line the pudding basin with cling film and cover its base and sides with overlapping brioche slices. Scoop the softened fruit into the basin and reserve the syrup and juices for later use.

Top the pudding with a slice of brioche and cover with cling film. Put a small plate over the top of the pudding and weigh down with a either a small weight from your scales or a couple of cans of beans, or whatever you happen to have in the cupboards.

Chill overnight in the fridge. Turn the pudding out of the bowl, peel off the cling film and slowly pour over the saved fruit juices to completely coat the brioche.

BITS & BOBS

Flavoured butters
Zest of an orange: great spread onto scones or muffins
Lemon zest: delicious on chicken or veal escalope
Lime: fantastic on tuna or any oily fish
Garlic: amazing on steak or warm crusty bread
Finely chopped mint leaves: fab to enhance spring veggies

Flavoured glazes
Squeeze either an orange, lime or lemon into a sieve over a bowl, then stir in about 75g of icing sugar. I put it into either a squeezy bottle or a disposable piping bag and drizzle over my warm bake for a lovely glaze.

Hot chocolate
Per person: heat 250ml milk in a saucepan to just under boiling point. Add a glug of double cream and 60g chopped dark chocolate. Take the pan off of the heat and whisk until the chocolate has melted and you have a lovely frothy top. Pour into a heatproof glass cup and add one, two, five or none of the toppings and enjoy.

Options for toppings:
a grating of fresh nutmeg
half a pinch of dried chilli flakes
a handful of marshmallows, mini or big depending on your preference
a nip of Baileys or something equally as decadent
1 Flake, crumbled
squirty cream in a can or whipped double cream

Easy strawberry jam
500g ripe strawberries, hulled
450g jam sugar

Tip the strawberries into a saucepan and crush with a fork. Add the sugar and give a good stir. Set the pan over a low to medium heat and bring to the boil, stirring to completely dissolve the sugar. Lower the heat and continue to cook at a gentle simmer for 5 minutes until the jam has thickened and will coat the back

of a spoon. Remove the pan from the heat and leave the jam to settle for 5 minutes, using a spoon to carefully skim any scum from the top of the jam. Pour into a bowl and leave to chill before eating.

Flavoured syrups
All these syrups make enough for a family-size cake or 12 cupcakes.

Orange or lemon and lime syrup
Squeeze the juice from either 1 large or 2 medium oranges, or 2–3 limes and 1 lemon. Pour the juice through a sieve into a small saucepan. Add 4 heaped tablespoons of caster sugar and 3 tablespoons of water. Bring to the boil, then reduce the heat to a simmer and continue to cook until the syrup has thickened and reduced by half. If the syrup is ready it should coat the back of a spoon.

Rosemary or thyme syrup
Pour a cup of water and a cup of sugar into a small saucepan, add a sprig of either rosemary or thyme and bring to the boil. Turn the heat down to a simmer and reduce until thickened enough to coat the back of a spoon. Remove the herbs before serving.

Chocolate syrup
Mix 2 teaspoons of cocoa into a paste with half a cup of water. Tip a cup of sugar and half a cup of water into a saucepan and bring to the boil. Add the cocoa paste and whisk until combined. Turn down the heat to a gentle simmer and continue to cook until the syrup has reduced by half.

Buttercream
Basic buttercream: this is enough to generously ice 12 cupcakes or 20 with a more modest amount.
250g unsalted butter, softened
1kg icing sugar
2–3 tbsp of milk

Beat the butter in the bowl of a free-standing mixer until smooth. Gradually add the icing sugar and milk and beat on a slow speed to combine. Beat for 10 minutes until soft and light, adding a little more

milk if necessary. For colouring buttercream I always use gel colours. Dip a cocktail stick into the pot, add to the beaten buttercream and mix until thoroughly combined. Gradually build up the colour intensity with more little dips if you need to. It's best to slowly build the colour up in the buttercream as you can't take the colour out once it's in!

Chocolate buttercream
Add 50g melted dark chocolate to the buttercream once you have added all of the icing sugar. Continue to beat until soft and light.

Lemon, orange or lime buttercream
Once you have added the icing sugar to the buttercream, add the finely grated zest of 1 or 2 fruits according to taste. Continue to beat until the buttercream is soft and light.

Buttercream with liqueur
Add 1–2 tablespoons of a sweet liqueur after adding the icing sugar to the buttercream.

Cream-cheese buttercream
Replace half of the butter with full-fat cream cheese.

Coffee buttercream
Add 1–2 teaspoons of strong coffee to the milk before adding to the buttercream.

Butterscotch buttercream
Heat 60g soft brown sugar, 60g unsalted butter and 60ml double cream in a small saucepan until the butter and sugar have dissolved, stirring all the time. Remove from the heat and leave to chill. Add 2–4 tablespoons of cooled butterscotch to the basic buttercream according to your taste. Any remaining butterscotch can be warmed and poured over ice cream.

Mixed peel paste
I really like the flavour of mixed peel in my baking but I can't stand the texture. So for years I have been processing mine to a paste, resulting in all the lovely taste and none of the pieces. Simply put a whole tub of mixed peel

into a food processor and blend until you have a smooth paste. Store in an airtight box or jar for use as and when needed.

Fruit smoothies

Tumble a handful of ice cubes and a punnet of soft fruits into a blender goblet. This can be anything from strawberries to raspberries and blueberries, or a mixture of all 3. Now you can add a skinned and cored small ripe pineapple or some fresh melon, 3 peeled kiwis, a large handful of grapes or any combination of these fruits, plus 2 large bananas and 1 large glass of fresh fruit juice (from a carton is fine). Blend everything together until smooth, pour into a serving jug and for full vitamin goodness, serve as soon as possible.

Herb teas

You will need:
**a large handful of fresh mint
half a sprig of rosemary
2 strips of lemon rind**

Using a large pestle and mortar or a big bowl and the end of a rolling pin, bash all the herbs until bruised but still intact, then put into the bottom of a cafetiere or the centre chamber of a teapot. Pour over boiling water and leave to stand for 5–8 minutes to infuse. Drink either warm or chilled, adding local honey to sweeten if you like.

Or try this combination using the same method as above:
**2 lemongrass sticks
a sprig of lemon verbena
a handful of fresh spearmint**

Sauces

For a really quick, easy dessert, take either a home-made chocolate chip or peanut butter cookie and place a scoop of vanilla ice cream on it, topped off with a simple sauce:

Chocolate sauce
Mix 100g chopped dark chocolate with 100ml double cream and melt in the microwave on a low setting. Stir until smooth and serve.

Raspberry sauce
Blend 200g of raspberries with 5 teaspoons of icing sugar and the juice of half an orange. Push through a sieve to remove the seeds and serve.

Strawberry sauce
Blend 200g of freshly washed and hulled strawberries with 4 teaspoons of icing sugar. Push through a sieve to remove the seeds and serve.

Top with either nuts or chocolate chips and for real dessert overload, some whipped cream!

Sticky sauces
Orange sauce
Peel and thinly slice 1 orange. Heat a knob of butter in a frying pan, add half a glass of orange juice and a teaspoon of caster sugar. Cook over a medium heat until reduced by half. Add the orange slices to warm through.

Blueberry and orange
Tip a punnet of blueberries into a saucepan, add the grated zest and juice of 1 orange and a small cup of sugar. Bring to the boil, turn down the heat to a gentle simmer and continue to cook until all of the blueberries have burst. Spoon into a jug and serve with pancakes.

Home-made tomato sauce
Plunge 8–10 tomatoes into boiling water and leave for 2 minutes. Slit the skins and peel. Roughly chop the tomato flesh and tip into a pan with 125g soft brown sugar and stir to combine. Add 2 tablespoons of white wine vinegar and a teaspoon of Worcestershire sauce and cook over a medium heat until the sauce has reduced down to a paste. Season with salt and freshly ground black pepper. Cool and spoon into a sterilized jar. It will keep for five days in the fridge.

Children's lollies
For children's lollies you could use either milk or white chocolate and top with mini marshmallows, Smarties and sugar sprinkles.

Canapes
Brush your bread circles with olive oil, sprinkle with rock salt and press into bun tins. Bake in a hot oven (220°C/425°F/Gas Mark 7) for about 7–8 minutes until golden and crisp. Leave to cool in the tins and then fill with your choice of fillings: maybe some ready-made crab cocktail or cream cheese whipped with lemon juice and topped with smoked salmon and a snip of fresh chives. Try goats' cheese and chutney or roast beef with horseradish mayonnaise. The choices are endless. For some more little canapés, thinly slice some 2-day-old bread, mozzarella and beef tomatoes. Line the centre of half the sliced bread with the cheese and tomato and top up with a few torn basil leaves. Top with the other slices of bread, trim off the crusts and slice into finger sandwiches. Heat the olive oil in a frying pan and gently fry the sandwiches until golden on each side. Drain on kitchen paper and serve.

Eggy Bread
Just beat an egg with a little splash of milk, add a flurry of cinnamon (oh all right, half a teaspoonful, but flurry sounded nicer) and some melted butter (about a tablespoon). Lay your slice of bread in the mixture then pop a frying pan onto a medium heat, add a splash of oil and a little butter and when it is hot pop in your eggy bread, cook for a couple of minutes on each side until it becomes golden and crispy: enjoy.

Lemon and Marscapone cream
Whip 150ml of double cream, fold in 100g marscapone cheese and 2 tablespoons of lemon curd and add icing sugar to taste (about 2 tsp).

Flavoured sugars
To add flavour to your sugar, just pour caster sugar into sterilized jam jars, and add one of the following, vanilla bean pods, cardamom pods, lemon grass, dried lavender flowers, dried rosemary sprigs and leave for about 3 weeks so that the sugar takes on the flavour.

INDEX